SCORE
SHAKE

Digital
SAT

Reading and Writing
Advanced

JUSTIN SONG
ADAM GRODEN

Claremont, Inc

SCORESHAKE.COM

Unlock Your Potential with SCORESHAKE.COM – Your Premier Digital SAT Test Prep Solution!
Experience our cutting-edge test platform on the website,
where students can take the Digital SAT practice tests with ease.

Boasting over 40 practice tests and more than 7,000 expertly crafted questions,
our online platform guarantees a significant improvement in students' scores,
regardless of their current performance level.

Bid farewell to confusion and uncertainty surrounding the new digital SAT format.
Let SCORESHAKE.COM demystify the process and guide you on the path to achieving your perfect score!

WHAT'S IN SCORESHAKE?

• 40+ Digital SAT Practice Tests.
• New tests updated Bi-weekly.
• Instant scoring and detailed explanations
• Engaging explanation video clips that unveil the secrets to tackling challenging SAT questions
• Comprehensive question banks for targeted practice – the surefire way to boost your score
• Adaptive learning technology that personalizes study plans based on individual needs
• Interactive, user-friendly interface for an enjoyable test prep experience

BENEFITS

• Improved test scores through almost unlimited practices
• Increased confidence and reduced test anxiety through test familiarity
• Convenient, flexible, and self-paced learning
• Access to expert tips and strategies
• Affordable pricing and multiple subscription options

ISBN 979-8-9883597-0-8

90000 >

9 798988 359708

CONTENTS

SCORE
SHAKE

scoreshake.com

Digital SAT
Practice Test #1

I

II

III

IV

V

Section 1, Module 1: Reading and Writing

32:00

Directions   Hide

Annotate   More

∨

The questions in this section address a number of important reading and writing skills. Each question includes one or more passages, which may include a table or graph. Read each passage and question carefully, and then choose the best answer to the question based on the text(s).

All questions in this section are multiple-choice with four answer choices. Each question has a single best answer.

Section 1, Module 1: Reading and Writing
Directions ∨

32:00
Hide

Annotate   More

The analysis of ancient DNA has shed light on the origins and movements of ancient populations, including the discovery of a previously unknown group of humans in the Philippines. Recent research suggests that this group of humans may have interbred with modern humans and _____ the genetic diversity of populations in Southeast Asia.

1

Which choice completes the text with the most logical and precise word or phrase?

(A) withdrawn from

(B) contributed to

(C) yielded to

(D) adhered to

SCORE SHAKE

Next

Section 1, Module 1: Reading and Writing
Directions ∨

32:00
Hide

Annotate   More

Magnetic fields play an important role in the formation and _____ of stars. These fields influence the structure of interstellar clouds, the star formation process, and the behavior of protostellar material as it collapses to form a star. Furthermore, magnetic fields are believed to be crucial in regulating the mass accretion rate of new material onto a protostar, and in the loss of material from the system during the star's lifetime.

2

Which choice completes the text with the most logical and precise word or phrase?

(A) evolution

(B) enlargement

(C) kindling

(D) procession

SCORE SHAKE

Back   Next

Section 1, Module 1: Reading and Writing

The rise of music streaming services has had a significant effect on the music industry. A vast library of music is now available to listeners all over the world, providing convenient and affordable access to a _____ of genres to users all over the world.

3

Which choice completes the text with the most logical and precise word or phrase?

- (A) saturation
- (B) plethora
- (C) congestion
- (D) superfluity

Section 1, Module 1: Reading and Writing

Investigating the relationships and biogeography of _____ plants offers a precise and comprehensive approach to understanding the evolutionary history of these ancient lineages. Conversely, traditional molecular analyses that rely on a limited number of gene regions are prone to underestimating the complexity of old species and their biogeography.

4

Which choice completes the text with the most logical and precise word or phrase?

- (A) contemporary
- (B) alluring
- (C) virulent
- (D) primordial

Criminal behavior is influenced by a complex interplay of psychological and social factors. For instance, studies have shown that personality disorders such as psychopathy and antisocial personality disorder, can increase the likelihood of engaging in criminal behavior. <u>Individuals with these disorders may exhibit traits such as impulsivity, aggression, and a lack of empathy, making it difficult for them to adhere to social norms and laws.</u> In addition, family background has been identified as a significant factor in predicting criminal behavior. Children who grow up in households characterized by poverty, neglect, abuse, and family conflict are more likely to engage in criminal activities later in life.

5

Which choice best describes the function of the underlined sentence in the text as a whole?

- (A) It expands on the claim made by the studies mentioned in the previous sentence.

- (B) It presents empirical evidence that criminal behavior is influenced by personality disorders such as psychopathy and antisocial personality disorder.

- (C) It contends that personality disorders do not contribute to criminal behavior, but rather the environment in which an individual grows up is solely responsible.

- (D) It suggests that individuals with personality disorders are more likely to adhere to social norms because of their heightened sense of societal expectations.

Back   Next

"*Vanitas of Earthly Delights*" is a poem by an anonymous poet.

Oh, foolish man, how proud thy heart
To think thy deeds will never part
From this world's fleeting glory vain
That withers like the summer's grain

Thy wealth, thy power, thy pomp and state
Are but illusions that await
The stroke of Time, which fells them low
And leaves thee empty, poor, and slow

Thus, learn to trust in things divine
And in thy heart let wisdom shine
For naught of earth shall e'er endure
But faith in God shall make thee sure.

6

Which choice best states the main purpose of the text?

- (A) To persuade individuals to adopt faith as their fundamental motivating principle in doing good deeds

- (B) To praise human innovation and hard work in achieving greater financial stability, wealth, and respect among peers

- (C) To contrast the pursuit of worldly possessions with the pursuit of intellectual fulfillment through learning

- (D) To convey a message of the transience and impermanence of worldly things such as wealth, power, and high status

Back   Next

Section 1, Module 1: Reading and Writing

Directions ∨

32:00
Hide

Annotate   More

Animal testing is a highly debated topic, with arguments both for and against its necessity in scientific advancement and medical treatments. The truth is that animal testing is not only inhumane but also unnecessary. Other methods such as computer models and cell cultures are more accurate and reliable in testing new medications and treatments. Additionally, differences in how humans and non-human animals respond to treatments make these tests useless. As a society, we need to move away from the outdated and cruel practice of animal testing and focus on alternative methods that are more humane and effective.

7

Which choice best states the main idea of the text?

- (A) Computer modeling is a highly efficient, cost-effective, and reliable alternative to cell cultures for testing new medications and treatments.

- (B) The practice of animal testing is outdated and unnecessary, and it should be replaced by more humane and accurate testing methods.

- (C) Animal testing cannot accurately forecast human reactions to medicines and remedies and should only be used when no other means is available.

- (D) Animal testing is essential for the progress of science and the creation of novel medicines and remedies.

SCORE SHAKE

Back   Next

Section 1, Module 1: Reading and Writing

Directions ∨

32:00
Hide

Annotate   More

Every moment, our brains are bombarded with information, from without and within. The eyes alone convey more than a hundred billion signals to the brain every second. The ears receive another avalanche of signals. Then there are the fragments of thoughts, conscious and unconscious, that <u>race</u> from one neuron to the next.

8

As used in the text, what does the word "race" most nearly mean?

- (A) step
- (B) attach
- (C) dash
- (D) throb

SCORE SHAKE

Back   Next

Text 1

The death penalty is viewed by some as a justified and necessary punishment for heinous crimes, such as murder. Proponents argue that it acts as a strong deterrent to potential offenders and ensures that they are permanently removed from society, thus preventing them from committing further crimes. Supporters also contend that capital punishment provides closure to the families of victims who have been subjected to unimaginable suffering.

Text 2

The death penalty is an archaic and inhumane method of punishment that has been demonstrated to have no impact on crime rates. Furthermore, it has the potential to execute individuals who are innocent, and it demonstrates racial and economic biases, with minorities and impoverished individuals more likely to receive death sentences. Life imprisonment without the possibility of parole is a more compassionate and equitable option that still guarantees the removal of violent offenders from society.

9

Based on the texts, how would the author of Text 2 most likely respond to the underlined statement in Text 1?

(A) By endorsing the idea that the implementation of the death penalty as a punishment for crimes has resulted in a significant reduction in crime rates compared to life imprisonment

(B) By comparing the effectiveness of life sentences and the death penalty on deterring crimes against minorities

(C) By highlighting evidence demonstrating that the death penalty is no more effective in deterring crime than the threat of life imprisonment

(D) By emphasizing that racial discrimination in the judicial system is a more significant issue than the death penalty's effectiveness as a measure of deterrence

SCORE SHAKE

Back   Next

Lord Jim is a novel by Joseph Conrad, originally published in 1900. A "ship chandler" sells equipment for ships and boats.

[The water-clerk's] work consists in racing under sail, steam, or oars against other water-clerks for any ship about to anchor, greeting her captain cheerily, forcing upon him a card—the business card of the ship-chandler—and on his first visit on shore piloting him firmly but without ostentation to a vast, cavern-like shop which is full of things that are eaten and drunk on board ship; where you can get everything to make her seaworthy and beautiful, from a set of chain-hooks for her cable to a book of gold-leaf for the carvings of her stern; and where her commander is received like a brother by a ship-chandler he has never seen before. There is a cool parlour, easy-chairs, bottles, cigars, writing implements, a copy of harbour regulations, and a warmth of welcome that melts the salt of a three months' passage out of a seaman's heart.

10

According to the text, what is the objective of the water clerk?

(A) It is to market the ship-chandler's store by disseminating the chandler's contact information and bringing his products to various ships.

(B) It is to be the first clerk to bring a captain to a chandler's where the captain is treated well and encouraged to make purchases.

(C) It is to visit different ports worldwide and offer essential items needed for the functioning of a vessel to sailors and captains.

(D) It involves creating and disseminating promotional material for a ship-chandler's store and ensuring its distribution.

SCORE SHAKE

Back   Next

1   1

Section 1, Module 1: Reading and Writing
Directions ∨

32:00
Hide

Annotate   More

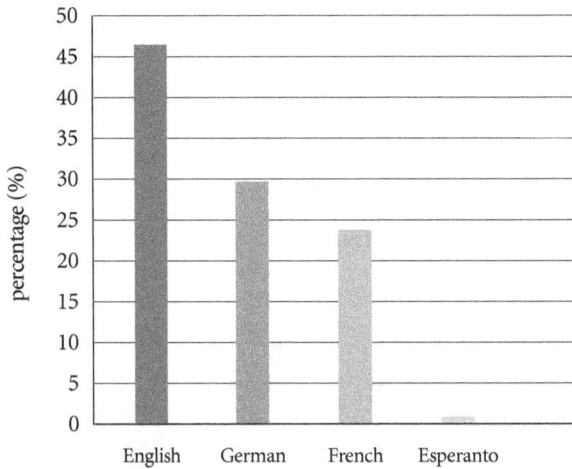

Second Languages of EU (EuroPean Union) Population

Esperanto is a constructed language introduced in the late 19th century by a Polish ophthalmologist named L.L. Zamenhof. The language was designed to be universal, fostering peace and understanding between different cultures. Despite its noble intentions, however, the number of people who use Esperanto regularly is relatively small. It is estimated that there are only a few thousand native speakers of Esperanto in the world and perhaps two million more with some knowledge of the language. Although Esperanto has never achieved the widespread adoption that its proponents had hoped for, it remains an essential symbol of the ideal of a universal language and a testament to the power of linguistic innovation.

11

Which choice best describes data from the graph that support the claim mentioned in the text?

(A) A considerable proportion of Esperanto speakers are young people who are motivated by a desire for global harmony.

(B) Compared to languages such as English, Esperanto has been learned only by a small population.

(C) As the popularity of Esperanto increases on social media, there has been a rise in the number of people learning the language.

(D) In Europe, more people prefer to study German compared to French as a second language.

Probiotics and prebiotics are beneficial bacteria and dietary fibers that may have positive effects on health. A recent study conducted by the University of Chicago Medical Center suggests that the combination of both probiotics and prebiotics is more effective than either supplement alone in improving the gut microbiome and reducing inflammation. Additionally, the study showed that supplementation with probiotics and prebiotics can lead to improved digestion, stronger immune system function, and a decreased risk of certain chronic diseases. These findings suggest that probiotics and prebiotics may be useful for maintaining gut health and overall health and well-being.

12

Which finding, if true, would most directly support the University's claim?

(A) Prebiotics may have a lasting impact by supporting the growth and diversity of beneficial bacteria when utilized independently of other supplements.

(B) Probiotics are commonly found in fermented foods like yogurt, kefir, kimchi, and sauerkraut.

(C) The effectiveness of probiotics can vary depending on the specific strain, dosage, and individual factors such as age, health status, and diet.

(D) Consumption of probiotics and prebiotics was associated with a reduced risk of depression in a study involving 2,000 adults.

Question 12 of 27 ⌃

Back   Next

The effects of parental divorce on child development have been the subject of extensive research over the years. Some researchers have suggested that divorce can have negative effects on children's emotional, behavioral, and academic outcomes, while others have proposed that the impact of divorce may depend on a variety of factors, such as the child's age, gender, and temperament, as well as the quality of the parent-child relationship both before and after the divorce. In particular, some researchers have hypothesized that children who experience high levels of conflict between their parents before the divorce may experience greater negative effects than those who come from families with lower levels of conflict.

13

Which statement, if true, would be most likely to support hypothesis of the researchers?

(A) Children who experienced high levels of conflict before the divorce experience serious undereating, while the children who experienced lower levels of conflict experience significant overeating.

(B) Children who experienced high levels of conflict before the divorce tend to be the subject of extensive research compared to children who experienced lower levels of conflict.

(C) Children who experienced high levels of conflict before the divorce may have more difficulty adjusting to co-parenting arrangements than children who experienced lower levels of conflict.

(D) Children who experienced high levels of conflict before the divorce may have the opportunity to reflect on their own values and gain greater self-awareness compared to children who experienced lower levels of conflict.

Term limits are a controversial issue in American politics. Supporters argue that they prevent the consolidation of power and the rise of political dynasties, while critics suggest they limit experienced lawmakers' ability to represent constituents. Higher rates of turnover in elected offices are a fact of the impact of term limits on political representation. This has both positive and negative effects, allowing for greater diversity of perspectives but also leading to a lack of continuity and experience among lawmakers. Term limits may also disproportionately impact certain demographic groups, such as women and minorities, who may have less access to political networks and resources necessary to mount successful campaigns. Overall, _____

14

Which choice most logically completes the text?

- (A) there is a widespread awareness and understanding of the potential benefits and drawbacks of term limits among the American public and political leaders.

- (B) term limits necessarily neutralize the legislative effectiveness by preventing lawmakers from gaining expertise and experience in their roles.

- (C) term limits are the most important factor influencing political representation of certain demographic groups.

- (D) an appraisal of term limits should take into account the advantages and disadvantages of the impact they have on political representation.

SCORE SHAKE

Back   Next

Hollywood, located in Los Angeles, California, is a world-renowned entertainment industry hub. It is where many of the world's biggest movies and television shows are made and where aspiring actors, directors, and producers come to pursue their dreams of making it big in the industry. The famous actor Tom Hanks _____ which was filmed in Hollywood and won several Academy Awards.

15

Which choice completes the text so that it conforms to the conventions of Standard English?

- (A) starred in the movie, "Forrest Gump"

- (B) starred in the movie "Forrest Gump"

- (C) starred in the movie "Forrest Gump,"

- (D) starred, in the movie "Forrest Gump,"

SCORE SHAKE

Back   Next

Section 1, Module 1: Reading and Writing

32:00
Hide

Annotate   More

Directions ⌄

The Hope Diamond is one of the most famous gemstones in the world, a large, blue diamond with a fascinating history. This 45.52-carat diamond has been rumored to have brought bad luck to its previous owners. Originally known as the Tavernier Blue, it was sold to King Louis XIV of _____ it was stolen during the French Revolution.

16

Which choice completes the text so that it conforms to the conventions of Standard English?

(A) France, later,

(B) France; later,

(C) France later;

(D) France, later

Section 1, Module 1: Reading and Writing

32:00
Hide

Annotate   More

Directions ⌄

Real estate prices in Japan have been rising because of a _____ a shortage of available properties. The government has implemented policies to control prices and encourage the development of affordable housing, but with the upcoming Tokyo Olympics and Paralympics, prices are expected to continue rising because of increased demand from investors.

17

Which choice completes the text so that it conforms to the conventions of Standard English?

(A) growing economy and burgeoning population, leading to

(B) growing economy, and burgeoning population, leading to

(C) growing economy and, burgeoning population, leading to

(D) growing economy and burgeoning population leading to

Influenced by the cultural and historical contexts in which they arose, _____ From the realism of the Renaissance to the abstraction of the 20th century, each movement was shaped by the societal and cultural forces surrounding it, resulting in unique expressions of artistic vision and creativity.

18

Which choice completes the text so that it conforms to the conventions of Standard English?

- (A) the era's values and beliefs are reflections of artistic movements and styles.

- (B) the values and beliefs of their time are reflected in artistic movements and styles.

- (C) artistic movements and styles reflect the values and beliefs of their time.

- (D) the reflection of the values and beliefs of their time stems from artistic movements and styles.

The impact of automation and artificial intelligence on employment and the workforce has been significant: job displacement and changes in the labor market, which have occurred as many jobs that were once performed by humans are now being done by _____ in areas such as programming and data analysis; and increased efficiency and productivity, which is the outcome of the implementation of automation and the use of AI.

19

Which choice completes the text so that it conforms to the conventions of Standard English?

- (A) machines, creation of a demand for new skills and training, which shows a considerable spike

- (B) machines; creation of a demand for new skills and training; which shows a considerable spike.

- (C) machines, creation of a demand for new skills and training; which shows a considerable spike

- (D) machines; creation of a demand for new skills and training, which shows a considerable spike

One of the fascinating areas of neuroscience research is the study of brain _____ brain's ability to change and adapt throughout a person's lifetime. Recent studies have shown that the adult brain is more adaptable than previously thought, with new neural connections being formed in response to environmental stimuli and learning.

20

Which choice completes the text so that it conforms to the conventions of Standard English?

(A) plasticity. The

(B) plasticity; the

(C) plasticity the

(D) plasticity: the

Parents must make various decisions while rearing their baby, such as feeding, sleeping arrangements, and safety measures. _____ it is essential to understand the baby's developmental needs and how they change over time. Factors like the baby's age, weight, and general health should be considered while making such decisions.

21

Which choice completes the text with the most logical transition?

(A) Hence,

(B) Moreover,

(C) Nevertheless,

(D) Next,

Mitch Albom is an acclaimed author, journalist, and philanthropist who captivates readers with his thought-provoking works. _____ his best-selling book, "Tuesdays with Morrie," sparks self-reflection and inspires readers to lead more meaningful lives. Albom's storytelling prowess, combined with his charitable endeavors, profoundly impacts countless lives.

22

Which choice completes the text with the most logical transition?

(A) Furthermore,

(B) Regardless,

(C) Namely,

(D) Above all,

Schizophrenia is a complex mental disorder characterized by hallucinations, delusions, and disorganized thinking, often disrupting daily functioning and relationships. _____ when individuals receive early diagnosis and treatment, their quality of life can improve significantly, enabling them to better manage their symptoms and maintain relationships. The importance of timely support and intervention cannot be overstated.

23

Which choice completes the text with the most logical transition?

(A) Conversely,

(B) Moreover,

(C) Similarly,

(D) Subsequently,

Section 1, Module 1: Reading and Writing

Directions ⌄

✎ Annotate   ⋮ More

While researching a topic, a student has taken the following notes:

- M.F.K. Fisher was the name used by an influential author who wrote primarily about food.
- She wrote more than 27 books and was known for her insightful, often humorous, prose.
- Her first book was a novel that was clearly based on her own life up to that point.
- Her third book was *Consider the Oyster*, which contained recipes in addition to information about the history of the oyster and oyster cuisine.
- She achieved considerable success with *How to Cook a Wolf*, a book published during World War II that, among other things, offered advice on how to eat well under wartime conditions.
- In 1942, she started working in Hollywood, writing jokes for entertainers.

24

The student wants to introduce M.F.K. Fisher to an audience who is unfamiliar with the author. Which choice most effectively uses relevant information from the notes to accomplish this goal?

(A) The third of M.F.K. Fisher's 27 books, *Consider the Oyster* contained recipes in addition to information about the history of the oyster and oyster cuisine.

(B) M.F.K. Fisher, who mostly wrote about food, was an influential author known for her insightful, often humorous, prose.

(C) Fisher's successful book *How to Cook a Wolf*, published during World War II, offered advice on how to eat well under wartime conditions, and in 1942, she started to work in Hollywood, writing jokes for entertainers.

(D) The first book by M.F.K. Fisher, an influential author who wrote primarily about food, was clearly based on her own life up to that point.

Question 24 of 27 ⌃

Back   Next

While researching a topic, a student has taken the following notes:

- Bioarchaeology is the study of human remains from archaeological sites.
- In children, dental development is typically used as part of the process of determining the age of death.
- Changes to certain bones, including ribs, are often analyzed to determine the age-at-death of adult remains.
- Not all bones follow the same stages of growth, making age determination difficult.
- Because of wear and tear on the skeletal bones of older people, age estimation is less precise.
- If precision is impossible, the bones are simply termed "young, "middle," or "old."

25

The student wants to emphasize the problems involved in using bioarchaeology to determine the age of human remains. Which choice most effectively uses relevant information from the notes to accomplish this goal?

(A) The wear and tear on the skeletal bones of older people as well as the fact that not all bones follow the same stages of growth can cause difficulties.

(B) In bioarchaeology, when it is impossible to precisely determine the age of human remains, the bones are simply termed "young, "middle," or "old."

(C) Dental development is typically used as part of the process of determining the age of death in children, and changes to bones, including ribs, are analyzed to determine the age-at-death of adult remains.

(D) Bioarchaeology, the study of human remains from archaeological sites, often involves examining changes to certain bones, including ribs, to determine the age-at-death of adult remains.

While researching a topic, a student has taken the following notes:

- There have been increasing calls for museums to return some of their artifacts to the descendants of the people from whom the artifacts were taken.
- An international group surveyed the residents of a town whose ancestors had many of their artifacts taken during period of colonization.
- These artifacts were stored and on display in a museum in another country.
- The residents were asked whether they wanted the items returned, kept at the museum, or loaned to the museum for a certain period.
- If they said that they wanted the items returned, they were asked if they wanted them all back and where they wanted the returned artifacts kept.
- The responses to the survey varied with the respondent's familiarity with the artifacts.

26

The student wants to present the aim of the survey. Which choice most effectively uses relevant information from the notes to accomplish this goal?

(A) The international group surveyed the residents of a town whose ancestors had many of their artifacts stored and and put on display in a museum in another country after the artifacts had been taken during a period of colonization.

(B) The responses to the survey varied with the respondent's familiarity with the artifacts that had been taken during a period of colonization.

(C) The international group wanted to determine where the residents of the town wanted the artifacts kept.

(D) There have been increasing calls for museums that store and display artifacts to return some of the artifacts to the descendants of the people from whom the artifacts were taken.

While researching a topic, a student has taken the following notes:

- Reptiles, including crocodiles, have legs that sprawl out to the side.
- They walk with a side-to-side motion.
- Dinosaurs, have legs positioned directly under their bodies, giving them an upright stance.
- Birds, dinosaurs, and crocodiles are descended from archosaurs.
- Archosaurs are considered the crown group of reptiles.
- Crocodile relatives are believed to have existed at the same time as, or even earlier than, dinosaurs.

27

The student wants to emphasize a similarity between dinosaurs and crocodiles. Which choice most effectively uses relevant information from the notes to accomplish this goal?

(A) Crocodiles are reptiles that walk with a side-to-side motion.

(B) Dinosaurs, which are descended from archosaurs, have legs positioned directly under their bodies, giving them an upright stance.

(C) Dinosaurs and crocodiles both are descended from the crown group of reptiles.

(D) Relatives of crocodiles, which have legs that sprawl out to the side, are believed to have existed at the same time as, or even earlier than, dinosaurs.

SCORE SHΔKE

Back

Practice Test Break

You can resume this practice test as soon as you're ready to move on. On test day, you'll wait until the clock counts down.

Take a Break

You may leave the room, but do not disturb students who are still testing.

Do not exit the app or close your device.

Testing won't resume until you return.

Follow these rules during the break:

1. Do not access your phone, smartwatch, textbooks, notes, or the internet.

2. Do not eat or drink in the test room.

3. Do not speak in the test room; outside the test room, do not discuss the exam with anyone.

Remaing Break Time:

9:52

Resume Testing

Section 1, Module 2: Reading and Writing

Annotate   More

A high-quality genome sequence of spinach provides a wealth of information. Specifically, it offers _____ flowering time regulation, which is important for crop yield and adaptation to changing environmental conditions. This thorough genome sequence provides a comprehensive view of the genetic basis of the regulation of spinach's time to flourish.

1

Which choice completes the text with the most logical and precise word or phrase?

- (A) opportunities for
- (B) results in
- (C) Insights into
- (D) anecdotes about

Section 1, Module 2: Reading and Writing

Annotate   More

Wildebeests are _____ creatures, often trekking over 1,000 miles in a typical year in search of food resources that shift according to the rainy season. During these seasonal movements, wildebeests are often seen in groups of hundreds or even thousands.

2

Which choice completes the text with the most logical and precise word or phrase?

- (A) itinerant
- (B) indigenous
- (C) subdued
- (D) nocturnal

Section 1, Module 2: Reading and Writing

Annotate   More

As _____ defender of the value of free trade, the esteemed ex-Senator Ben Sasse is frequently solicited to deliver speeches across the globe, exalting the manifold benefits of open commerce. Sasse's orations, lauded for their unparalleled powers of persuasion, have been known even to sway the most vehement opponents of free trade.

3

Which choice completes the text with the most logical and precise word or phrase?

- (A) an antagonistic
- (B) a cavalier
- (C) an abrupt
- (D) a stalwart

SCORE SHAKE

Back   Next

Section 1, Module 2: Reading and Writing

Annotate   More

Throughout the Indian independence movement, Mahatma Gandhi distinguished himself as a _____ pacifist who resolutely defied governmental authority, albeit never resorting to physical aggression. The ideology of nonviolent resistance, which Gandhi ardently championed, has served as a wellspring of inspiration for numerous other social and political movements across the globe, including the American civil rights movement.

4

Which choice completes the text with the most logical and precise word or phrase?

- (A) fickle
- (B) moribund
- (C) recalcitrant
- (D) spurious

SCORE SHAKE

Back   Next

The Ukra-Russo war has significantly affected the supply and demand of various goods and services. The war has destroyed many infrastructures and affected the region's movement of goods and services. The production of agricultural products such as wheat, corn, and barley has been hindered due to the lack of access to farming lands, disruptions in transportation, and the displacement of farmers. This has increased the prices of these commodities, affecting the purchasing power of consumers. The conflict has also impacted the energy sector, disrupting oil and gas supply to countries that depend on Russia for their energy needs. This has resulted in price increases, instability in the energy markets, and economic instability throughout the region.

5

Which choice best states the main purpose of the text?

(A) To explain how the Ukra-Russo war has affected the supply and demand of various goods and services in the region

(B) To emphasize the greater impact of the war on the agricultural sector than on the energy sector

(C) To demonstrate that the economic instability in the region is a consequence of volatility in the energy market

(D) To argue that economic stability in Europe has improved significantly due to the strong performance of the energy and agricultural sectors

SCORE SHΛKE

Question 5 of 27 ∧

Back   Next

It is probable that the assemblages of sauropod dinosaurs constituted some of the most densely populated groups of terrestrial creatures that have ever roamed the Earth. These extensive multitudes, potentially comprising a hundred individuals or more, could have stretched for miles and included members exhibiting a diverse range of ages and sizes, thereby indicating the presence of complex social structures. Establishing these populous herds may have shielded the dinosaurs from potential predators and facilitated more effective access to food and resources. By examining fossilized sauropod trackways, paleontologists have been afforded the opportunity to reconstruct the migratory patterns, unveiling the propensity for these creatures to traverse linear paths or adhere to predetermined courses in pursuit of food. Studying these primordial herds illuminates the behavioral tendencies and social organizations of dinosaurs and offers invaluable insights into the ecological dynamics that pervaded the prehistoric world.

6

Which choice best states the main idea of the text?

(A) The consistency of the trackways and the presence of different sized footprints suggest that the herds were composed of individuals of different ages and sizes.

(B) Studying the large, intricate social groups formed by Sauropod dinosaurs has increased our understanding of the prehistoric world.

(C) Without comprehending the behavior and social structure of dinosaurs, discovering more about the ecology of the prehistoric world is nearly impossible.

(D) Sauropods could safeguard their resources against predators and marauders by forming herds of colossal size.

SCORE SHΛKE

Question 6 of 27 ∧

Back   Next

The following text is from American poet Madison Julius Cawein's poem "*Rest*."

Under the brindled beech,
Deep in the mottled shade,
Where the rocks hang in reach
Flower and ferny blade,
Let him be laid.

Here will the brooks, that rove
Under the mossy trees,
Grave with the music of
Underworld melodies,
Lap him in peace.

Here will the winds, that blow
Out of the haunted west,
Gold with the dreams that glow
There on the heaven's breast,
Lull him to rest.

Here will the stars and moon,
Silent and far and deep,
Old with the mystic rune
Of the slow years that creep,
Charm him with sleep.

7

Which choice best describes the overall structure of the text?

- (A) Each stanza describes how the man that has been laid to rest has had a virtuous life.

- (B) The first stanza presents a poignant situation that is developed in the remaining stanzas.

- (C) The first two stanzas describe the setting, while the last two stanzas describe the man that has been laid to rest.

- (D) Each stanza after the introductory stanza describes how the natural setting will favorably affect the man that has been laid to rest.

SCORE SHAKE

Back   Next

Studies have shown that the hippocampus, a brain region in the medial temporal lobe, plays a critical role in spatial navigation and memory. Researchers have found that special "place cells" in the hippocampus become activated when an individual is in a specific location in their environment, creating a cognitive map of the space. Additionally, studies have shown that the hippocampus is important for the consolidation of memories, the process by which newly acquired information is transferred from short-term to long-term memory storage. Understanding the neural mechanisms underlying spatial memory has important implications for a range of applications, from improving spatial navigation in individuals with cognitive impairments to developing new approaches for treating memory-related disorders such as Alzheimer's disease.

8

According to the text, what is the role of the hippocampus in memory consolidation?

- (A) The hippocampus triggers the creation of place cells used in long-term memories.

- (B) The hippocampus assists the medial temporal lobe in creating a cognitive map of spatial navigation and memory.

- (C) The hippocampus mediates the transfer of recently acquired information from short-term to long-term memory storage, a process called memory consolidation.

- (D) The hippocampus plays a direct role in treating memory-related disorders such as Alzheimer's disease.

SCORE SHAKE

Back   Next

Section 1, Module 2: Reading and Writing

32:00
Hide

Annotate More

Directions ⌄

Text 1

Throughout history, philosophers, teachers, and scientists from diverse times and cultures have proposed the concept of <u>duality</u>, which refers to the two-sidedness of human nature. Duality suggest that there are two distinct ways of understanding and knowing the world. Examples include thinking and feeling, intellect and intuition, and objective analysis and subjective insight.

Text 2

Early humans required independent use of their arms while hunting and foraging, leading to an asymmetric arrangement between brain hemispheres that differed from symmetric activities like swimming or walking. As one arm or hand was used more frequently, the hemispheres specialized further and progressed in tandem over thousands of years.

9

Based on the texts, how would the author of text 2 would most likely explain the "duality" mentioned in text 1?

- (A) By asserting that the notion of duality cannot be proven without considering evidence drawn from philosophy

- (B) By explaining the duality of human nature and thought as related to the asymmetry of the brain

- (C) By viewing the development of the two-sidedness of human beings as a result of our ancestors' engagement in activities such as swimming or walking

- (D) By incorporating hunting and foraging as an additional illustration of duality, akin to the pairing of intellect and intuition.

SCORE
SHAKE

Back   Next

Published in 1859, *A Tale of Two Cities* is a novel by Charles Dickinson that portrays the lives of both English and French characters amidst the tumultuous backdrop of the French Revolution. In the novel, the character Carlton is portrayed as capricious as when Dickinson writes of the character: _____.

10

Which quotation from "*A Tale of Two Cities*" most effectively illustrates the claim?

Ⓐ "The old Sydney Carton of old Shrewsbury School, said Stryver, nodding his head over him as he reviewed him in the present and the past, the old seesaw Sydney. Up one minute and down the next; now in spirits and now in despondency!"

Ⓑ "Carlton, said his friend, squaring himself at him with a bullying air, as if the fire-grate had been the furnace in which sustained endeavour was forged, and the one delicate thing to be done for the old Sydney Carton of old Shrewsbury School…"

Ⓒ "Oh, botheration! Returned Sydney, with a lighter and more good-humoured laugh, don't you be moral!"

Ⓓ "Climbing to a high chamber in a well of houses, he threw himself down in his clothes on a neglected bed, and its pillow was wet with wasted tears."

NATIONAL SPENDING ON INFRASTRUCTURE
BY COUNTRY

	US	Germany	Canada	Japan
1940	3.1%	2.9%	2.0%	4.0%
1950	3.2%	2.2%	3.5%	2.2%
1960	4.0%	3.5%	3.8%	4.3%
1970	3.0%	4.1%	4.7%	4.5%
1980	3.5%	3.7%	4.5%	3.7%
1990	3.6%	4.0%	4.9%	3.5%
2000	4.0%	4.0%	4.3%	4.0%
2010	3.0%	4.0%	4.5%	5.0%

PRECENT OF GDP SPENT

The United States' infrastructure spending has been inadequate for several years compared to countries like Germany, Canada, and Japan. In recent years, infrastructure in the US has deteriorated due to underinvestment and deferred maintenance. The country's infrastructure ranks 13th in the world, behind countries like Germany, Canada, and Japan. These countries invest a much higher proportion of their GDP in infrastructure than does the US, allowing them to have a much higher quality of infrastructure. Experts have estimated that the US needs to spend approximately $4.5 trillion to bring its infrastructure up to a safe and efficient standard. The lack of infrastructure investment hinders economic growth and endangers public safety. The US government must increase its investment in infrastructure to improve the quality of life for its citizens and remain competitive on the global stage.

11

Which choice best describes data from the table that support the argument made in the text?

(A) Since the 1960s, the percentage of GDP that the US has allocated to infrastructure spending has consistently been lower than that of Germany, Canada, and Japan.

(B) Apart from the 2010, Canada has consistently surpassed Japan in terms of percentage of GDP allocated to infrastructure spending since the 1970.

(C) In 2010, the US spent at least 1.0% less of its GDP on infrastructure than did Germany, Canada, and Japan.

(D) In 1990, the US exceeded Japan in terms of percentage of GDP spent on infrastructure.

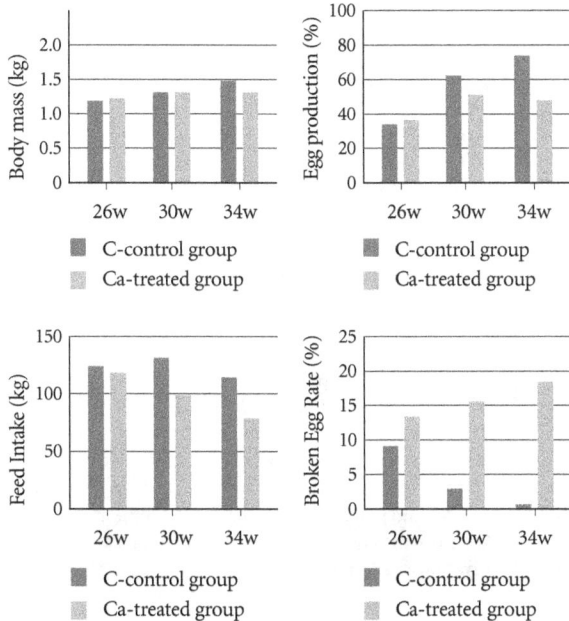

Cage layer fatigue is a condition that affects egg-laying hens due to their intensive confinement in battery cages, leading to an inability to engage in natural behaviors. Calcium deficiency in their feed is another common cause of this condition, resulting in loss of structural bone and increased fragility. Research conducted by S.C. Zhao et al. aimed to investigate the effect of low-calcium diets on egg quality. The study used 72 laying hens divided into two groups at 22 weeks, with one group (the "treated birds") receiving low calcium while the control group received normal calcium levels until 34 weeks. The research team concluded that egg-laying hens that were fed a low-calcium diet had reduced feed consumption and egg production, which ultimately led to a negative impact on the quality of eggs they produced.

12

Which choice best describes data from the graphs that support researchers' conclusion?

(A) At 30 and 34 weeks, the treated birds had a higher rate of broken eggs compared to the control group.

(B) At 26 weeks, there was no noteworthy contrast in body mass, feed intake, and egg output between the treated birds and the control group.

(C) After 34 weeks, birds on a normal diet showed a significant increase in body weight, feed consumption, and egg production.

(D) At 26 weeks, the birds fed a low-calcium diet exhibited a lower rate of broken eggs compared to birds on a normal diet.

Globalization has had a significant impact on economic development around the world. The increased interconnectedness of global markets has created new opportunities for trade and investment, allowing countries to specialize in the production of goods and services in which they have a comparative advantage. This has led to increased efficiency and productivity, driving economic growth and reducing poverty in many developing countries. However, critics of globalization point to its association with rising income inequality and job displacement in some countries, as the benefits of increased trade and investment are not always distributed evenly. Additionally, some have argued that globalization has led to a race to the bottom in terms of labor and environmental standards, as companies seek to reduce costs and increase profits. Based on the previous information, it can be concluded that some critics of globalization believe that _____.

13

Which choice most logically completes the text?

(A) compared to the economic prosperity brought on by globalization, factors such as education, infrastructure, and social policies are less significant in terms of their contribution to societal value

(B) globalization has brought benefits to many countries engaged in international trade, with the benefits being distributed relatively evenly among the countries

(C) globalization has led to a decrease in innovation and technological advancement in certain countries due to the specialization in goods and services in which these countries have a comparative advantage

(D) policies and regulations need to be implemented to ensure the equitable allocation of globalization's advantages among various groups and areas

The psychology of mindfulness-based stress reduction therapy, a form of meditation and yoga that combines mindfulness techniques to help individuals manage stress, pain, and illness, has been studied extensively in recent years. The results of the studies have been encouraging: the therapy has been shown to be effective in reducing stress and improving overall mental health. In particular it was found that mindfulness helps individuals develop greater awareness of their thoughts and feelings, which can help them manage their emotions more effectively and respond more skillfully to stressors in their lives. One study published in the journal Mindfulness in 2019 claimed that mindfulness-based stress reduction therapy is associated with significant improvement in overall levels of psychological distress, anxiety, and depression.

14

What evidence, if true, directly supports the claim made by the authors of the study published in Mindfulness?

(A) Mindfulness-based stress reduction therapy involves guided meditation, body scanning, and mindful breathing exercises designed to help participants cultivate greater awareness of their thoughts, feelings, and bodily sensations.

(B) Participants who received mindfulness-based stress reduction therapy report worsening symptoms of psychological distress, anxiety, and depression compared to a control group.

(C) Participants who received mindfulness-based stress reduction therapy showed signs of improved coping skills, resilience, and emotional well-being.

(D) Mindfulness-based stress reduction therapy has been shown to reduce inflammation markers in the body, which may help lower the risk of chronic diseases.

The Grand Canyon is one of the most iconic geological landmarks in the world, renowned for its stunning vistas and unique rock formations. A steep-sided canyon carved by the Colorado River, the canyon exposes over two billion years of Earth's geological history. It's a geologist's paradise, with rock formations ranging from Precambrian-era rocks at the bottom of the canyon to relatively young rock formations at the top. Using radiometric dating techniques, scientists have developed a keen understanding of the geologic history of the region. For example, the Vishnu Basement Rocks, which are the oldest rocks in the canyon, are estimated to be around 1.84 billion years old. The geologists who study the rock formations at the Grand Canyon would suggest that _____.

15

Which choice most logically completes the text?

(A) the cross-section of the Grand Canyon helps scientists to better understand geological processes over long span of time

(B) the Colorado River is the most crucial element that geologists should consider in understanding the formation of the Grand Canyon because the Colorado River solely carved the Grand Canyon

(C) because of the well-preserved rock formations exposing over two billion years of Earth's geological past, the Grand Canyon's geological history is fully understood

(D) the rock formations ranging from Precambrian-era rocks allow scientists to learn more about the evolution of living organisms

SCORE SHAKE

Question 15 of 27 ⌃

Back   Next

Located at the center of London is Buckingham Palace, the official residence of the British monarchy. The impressive architecture and expansive gardens symbolize the wealth and influence of the royal family. Visitors are granted the opportunity to partake in guided tours of the _____, offering a glimpse into the remarkable furnishings and priceless art collections within.

16

Which choice completes the text so that it conforms to the conventions of Standard English?

(A) palace's opulent state rooms'

(B) palaces opulent state rooms'

(C) palace's opulent state rooms

(D) palaces' opulent state rooms

SCORE SHAKE

Question 16 of 27 ⌃

Back   Next

Section 1, Module 2: Reading and Writing

Directions ∨

32:00
Hide

✎
Annotate

⋮
More

Gothic literature, a fascinating genre, captivates readers with its eerie atmosphere. It probes into the human psyche, exploring emotions of fear, horror, and desire. Key elements—dark, brooding settings, such as haunted mansions; tortured, enigmatic protagonists, like tormented _____ exemplified by star-crossed lovers; and ghostly apparitions, including specters and phantoms—converge to create an enthralling narrative.

17

Which choice completes the text so that it conforms to the conventions of Standard English?

(A) antiheroes, forbidden romance,

(B) antiheroes; forbidden romance,

(C) antiheroes, forbidden romance:

(D) antiheroes: forbidden romance

Civil engineering shapes the world by designing and constructing vital infrastructure. Civil engineers leave an indelible mark on society, from bridges and highways to dams and water treatment plants. By optimizing resources and sustainability, _____

18

Which choice completes the text so that it conforms to the conventions of Standard English?

Ⓐ ensuring the longevity and efficiency of our infrastructure and fostering safer, more resilient communities for generations to come are the primary goals of these professionals

Ⓑ these professionals ensure the longevity and efficiency of our built environment, fostering safer, more resilient communities for generations to come.

Ⓒ these professionals' ensuring of the longevity and efficiency of our built environment that fosters safer, more resilient communities for generations to come is their main goal.

Ⓓ the primary goal of these professionals is to ensure the longevity and efficiency of our built environment, which in turn fosters safer, more resilient communities for generations to come.

The enthralling world of marine biology unlocks the secrets of oceanic ecosystems and the diverse life forms that inhabit Earth's vast oceans. Researchers, driven by their passion for discovery, work tirelessly to understand the complex relationships between marine organisms and their _____ not only enhancing our appreciation of the natural world but also helping to preserve delicate marine ecosystems for generations to come.

19

Which choice completes the text so that it conforms to the conventions of Standard English?

(A) environments, and their findings

(B) environments, their findings

(C) environments; their findings

(D) environments. Their findings

Back　　Next

Compared to that of other management thinkers, _____ Widely regarded as the "Father of Modern Management," Drucker transformed how businesses operate by emphasizing the importance of goals, innovation, and effective leadership. His prolific writings and teachings have left a lasting impact, inspiring generations of managers and entrepreneurs worldwide.

20

Which choice completes the text so that it conforms to the conventions of Standard English?

(A) Peter Drucker stands unmatched in his influence on modern management principles.

(B) modern management principles have been profoundly shaped by Peter Drucker's unparalleled influence.

(C) Peter Drucker, in his influential role, has left an unparalleled mark on modern management principles.

(D) Peter Drucker's influence on modern management principles remains unparalleled.

Back　　Next

Researchers explore the complexities of emotions, cognition, and behavior _____ the human mind, often employing groundbreaking techniques to unlock the mysteries of our most powerful organ.

21

Which choice completes the text so that it conforms to the conventions of Standard English?

(A) better understands

(B) better understood

(C) is better understanding

(D) to better understand

The advent of technology has undoubtedly revolutionized our lives, making information and communication more accessible than ever before. It has also introduced _____ from individuals struggling to maintain healthy boundaries with technology usage to the ever-evolving landscape of cybersecurity threats that target sensitive personal and corporate information, these challenges manifest in various forms.

22

Which choice completes the text so that it conforms to the conventions of Standard English?

(A) new challenges, however;

(B) new challenges; however,

(C) new challenges, however,

(D) new challenges however

Physical exercise is essential for maintaining overall health and well-being, as it promotes cardiovascular fitness, strengthens muscles, and enhances mental clarity. _____ a balanced diet that includes a variety of fruits, vegetables, lean proteins, and whole grains is crucial for providing the body with the necessary nutrients and energy to function optimally. Together, these two pillars of a healthy lifestyle work synergistically to improve and sustain our quality of life.

23

Which choice completes the text with the most logical transition?

(A) As a result,

(B) Previously,

(C) Likewise,

(D) However,

Once considered a rare skill, whistling has now evolved into a competitive art form. _____ participants are mastering complex melodies and intricate techniques, captivating audiences worldwide. This newfound appreciation has revitalized the craft, transforming it into a harmonious blend of tradition and innovation.

24

Which choice completes the text with the most logical transition?

(A) Similarly,

(B) However,

(C) Notwithstanding,

(D) Increasingly,

The genome is a highly intricate and dynamic structure that encodes the entirety of an organism's genetic information within its DNA. Despite its complexity, remarkable strides have been made in the field of genomics that have enabled scientists to sequence and analyze genomes with unprecedented precision and detail. _____ elucidating the functional significance of specific genes and the regulatory mechanisms that govern their expression remains a highly complex and multifaceted undertaking.

25

Which choice completes the text with the most logical transition?

(A) Still,

(B) Indeed,

(C) In addition,

(D) Therefore,

SCORE SHAKE

Question 25 of 27 ∧

Back   Next

Section 1, Module 2: Reading and Writing

Directions ∨

32:00
Hide

Annotate   More

While researching a topic, a student has taken the following notes:

- Ellen Taaffe Zwillich is an American composer, the first woman to win the Pulitzer Prize for Music.
- She received the award for her Symphony No. 1.
- The piece was commissioned by the American Composers Orchestra.
- As with many of her pieces, nearly all the material is developed from the music at the beginning of the piece.
- She was the first person to occupy the Composer's Chair at Carnegie Hall.
- She has written four other symphonies.

26

The student wants to introduce Zwillich and her Symphony No. 1 to an audience that is unfamiliar with the work and its composer. Which choice most effectively uses relevant information from the notes to accomplish this goal?

(A) As with many of her pieces, Ellen Taaffe Zwillich, the first woman to win the Pulitzer Prize for Music, wrote four other symphonies developed from the music at the beginning of the pieces.

(B) Zwillich received the Pulitzer Prize for Music, and later wrote four other symphonies.

(C) Zwillich is the first woman to win the Pulitzer Prize for Music, and the first person to occupy the Composer's Chair at Carnegie Hall.

(D) Ellen Taaffe Zwillich, an American composer, develops nearly all the material in the Pulitzer Prize-winning composition from the music at the beginning of the piece as she does with many of her pieces.

Section 1, Module 2: Reading and Writing

Directions ⌄

Annotate   More

While researching a topic, a student has taken the following notes:

- Thirty medical school students who suffered from back pain volunteered to take part in a study.
- The students were split into three groups of ten.
- Over six weeks, each group was given a separate treatment for back pain: a medicine applied to their skin, a different medicine given as a pill, or physical therapy.
- At the start and again at the end of the six weeks, the students were asked to rate their perceived level of back pain.
- The difference between starting and ending ratings for each student was labeled "the differential."
- The differential values were published by the school in an article in the school's newspaper.

27

The student wants to emphasize the aim of the study. Which choice most effectively uses relevant information from the notes to accomplish this goal?

(A) The study was designed to show which treatment for back pain caused the students to give the lowest rating of their perceived level of back pain.

(B) The medical school students were given a separate treatment for back pain: a medicine applied to their skin, a different medicine given as a pill, or physical therapy.

(C) The school wanted to show the difference in perceived back pain for each treatment over a six-week period.

(D) The students who suffered from back pain were split into three groups of ten and asked to rate their perceived level of back pain at the start and end of a six-week period.

No.	Answer	Question Type
		TEST 1 Module 1
1	B	Text Completion
2	A	Text Completion
3	B	Text Completion
4	D	Text Completion
5	A	Function
6	D	Purpose / Poem
7	B	Main Idea
8	C	Vocabulary in Context
9	C	Cross-Text
10	B	Direct Comprehension / Literature
11	B	Command of Evidence / Quantitative
12	D	Command of Evidence / Textual
13	C	Command of Evidence / Textual
14	D	Inference
15	C	Conventions of Standard English
16	B	Conventions of Standard English
17	A	Conventions of Standard English
18	C	Conventions of Standard English
19	D	Conventions of Standard English
20	D	Conventions of Standard English
21	A	Transition
22	C	Transition
23	A	Transition
24	B	Note Summary
25	A	Note Summary
26	C	Note Summary
27	C	Note Summary

No.	Answer	Question Type
		TEST 1 Module 2
1	C	Text Completion
2	A	Text Completion
3	D	Text Completion
4	C	Text Completion
5	A	Main Purpose
6	B	Main Idea
7	D	Structure / Poem
8	C	Direct Comprehension
9	B	Cross-Text
10	A	Command of Evidence / Literature
11	C	Command of Evidence / Quantitative
12	A	Command of Evidence / Quantitative
13	D	Inference
14	C	Command of Evidence / Textual
15	A	Inference
16	C	Conventions of Standard English
17	B	Conventions of Standard English
18	B	Conventions of Standard English
19	B	Conventions of Standard English
20	D	Conventions of Standard English
21	D	Conventions of Standard English
22	A	Conventions of Standard English
23	C	Transition
24	D	Transition
25	A	Transition
26	D	Note Summary
27	C	Note Summary

DIGITAL SAT Advanced SCORING CHART
Raw score to Score Conversion Chart

Raw Score	Score	Incorrect	Score
54	800	26	530
53	770	25	530
52	740	24	510
51	730	23	510
50	710	22	490
49	710	21	480
48	690	20	480
47	680	19	460
46	680	18	450
45	670	17	430
44	660	16	400
43	650	15	380
42	630	14	360
41	630	13	340
40	620	12	330
39	620	11	310
38	620	10	300
37	610	9	280
36	600	8	260
35	600	7	260
34	590	6	250
33	590	5	240
32	580	4	220
31	580	3	200
30	570	2	200
29	560	1	200
28	550	0	200
27	540		

Digital SAT
Practice Test #II

Section 1, Module 1: Reading and Writing

32:00
Hide

Annotate More

The questions in this section address a number of important reading and writing skills. Each question includes one or more passages, which may include a table or graph. Read each passage and question carefully, and then choose the best answer to the question based on the text(s).

All questions in this section are multiple-choice with four answer choices. Each question has a single best answer.

Section 1, Module 1: Reading and Writing

Directions ⌄

32:00
Hide

Annotate

More

Critics of former British Prime Minister Winston Churchill complained that he too often acted _____, choosing his strategies without much consideration, leading to decisions that were at times both controversial and divisive among his peers and the public.

1

Which choice completes the text with the most logical and precise word or phrase?

- (A) sensibly
- (B) suspiciously
- (C) promptly
- (D) arbitrarily

Section 1, Module 1: Reading and Writing

Directions ⌄

32:00
Hide

Annotate

More

Despite the United States' efforts to provide Colombia with financial aid and military assistance to _____ drug trafficking, the production and trafficking of cocaine and heroin continue to thrive. In 2019 alone, the Colombian government reported a record-high production of over 1,137 metric tons of cocaine.

2

Which choice completes the text with the most logical and precise word or phrase?

- (A) facilitate
- (B) combat
- (C) administer
- (D) rebut

Ecological, political, and socioeconomic values intersect and sometimes conflict. Only recently have scientists from academia, industry, and government begun to quantify the trade-offs involved in renewable energy development. Success in this important field depends on affected parties _____ on issues such as wildlife protection and economic costs.

3

Which choice completes the text with the most logical and precise word or phrase?

- (A) supplanting
- (B) subverting
- (C) resigning
- (D) compromising

Positive reinforcement and open communication have been shown to be successful in fostering a nurturing learning environment. Developmental psychologists frequently assert that shouting at children is _____ and an unsuitable approach for facilitating learning. By promoting a sense of trust and emotional security, children are more likely to respond positively to guidance and instruction.

4

Which choice completes the text with the most logical and precise word or phrase?

- (A) inefficacious
- (B) diagnostic
- (C) discretionary
- (D) therapeutic

By the close of the 18th century, science had made remarkable strides in advancing humanity's understanding of the world and our own physical characteristics. It was at this point that people began to wonder if science could similarly further our knowledge of society.

5

As used in the text, what does the word "further" most nearly mean?

(A) distance

(B) enhance

(C) impede

(D) flaunt

Roasting coffee is a fascinating craft that transforms raw, green coffee beans into the aromatic, flavorful delights we know and love. This intricate process requires a delicate balance of temperature, time, and intuition as roasters carefully monitor the beans' progression through various stages. As the beans heat up, they undergo the Maillard reaction, which unleashes a symphony of complex flavors and enticing aromas. Observing the beans' color changes, roasters listen for the audible "cracks" that signal crucial milestones. Mastering the art of coffee roasting is a journey, with each batch revealing nuances that contribute to the perfect cup of coffee.

6

Which choice best describes the function of the underlined sentence in the text as a whole?

(A) It illustrates the transformation of raw, green coffee beans into fragrant, roasted ones.

(B) It celebrates the complexity and elegance inherent in the craft of coffee roasting.

(C) It highlights how the roaster's understanding evolves through the continuous learning process.

(D) It conveys the challenge involved in attaining expertise in the art of coffee bean roasting.

World War II played a pivotal role in lifting the United States out of the grips of the Great Depression. As the conflict escalated, the demand for military equipment, vehicles, and supplies skyrocketed. This surge in production needs led to a dramatic expansion of the American industrial sector, generating millions of jobs for those who had been struggling to make ends meet during the Depression. The war also spurred technological innovations that would have lasting impacts on the economy. In effect, the United States transitioned from a casualty of a bleak period of economic stagnation to a bustling powerhouse, laying the foundation for post-war prosperity and solidifying its position as a global leader.

7

Which choice best states the main purpose of the text?

(A) To explore the way the US industrial sector responded to the surge in production needs for military equipment and provisions

(B) To show that the ending of the Great Depression in the United States was considerably impacted by the events of World War II

(C) To emphasize the importance of World War II in elevating the United States out of the Great Depression in comparison to the contribution of technological innovation

(D) To illustrate how the World War II-induced Great Depression enabled the United States to solidify its position as a global leader

The following text is from Robert Burns' 1771 poem "*Handsome Nell.*"

> Once I lov'd a bonie lass,
> Ay, and I love her still;
> And whilst that virtue warms my breast,
> I'll love my handsome Nell.
>
> A gaudy dress and gentle air
> May slightly touch the heart;
> But it's innocence and modesty
> That polishes the dart.
>
> 'Tis this in Nelly pleases me,
> 'Tis this enchants my soul;
> For absolutely in my breast
> She reigns without control.

8

Which choice best states the main purpose of the text?

(A) To describe the characteristics that the speaker believes separate his beloved from other women

(B) To boast of the qualities that the speaker believes only he sees in the woman he loves

(C) To explain that the speaker is helplessly in love with Nell, though she does not feel the same

(D) To reminisce about a woman that the speaker loved when he was much younger

Text 1

The importance of environmental factors in shaping human development and behavior is undeniable, but genetics still provide the foundation upon which these environmental influences act. While nurturing plays a role in molding individuals, the influence of nature cannot be overlooked, as genetic predispositions and inherent traits can determine how people react and adapt to their environment. Furthermore, the interplay between genetics and environmental factors is complex, with both aspects working together to ultimately shape human behavior and development.

Text 2

Environmental factors have an undeniable impact on human development and behavior. <u>The experiences we have, the people we interact with, and the resources available to us all work together to shape who we become.</u> Our upbringing, education, and socio-economic background play a critical role in molding our character, values, and belief systems, ultimately influencing our behavior throughout our lives.

9

Based on the texts, how would the author of Text 1 most likely respond to the underlined statement in Text 2?

(A) By arguing that genetics alone can shape human development

(B) By asserting that no environmental factor can heavily affect human behavior

(C) By suggesting that innate qualities play as significant a role as external factors

(D) By explaining that genetic and environmental interplay is simple and straightforward

---

First published in 1890, *An Occurrence at Owl Creek Bridge* is a short story written by Ambrose Bierce.

Peyton Farquhar was a well-to-do planter, of an old and highly respected Alabama family. Being a slave-owner, and, like other slave-owners, a politician, he was naturally an original secessionist and ardently devoted to the Southern cause. Circumstances had prevented him from taking service with the gallant army that had fought the disastrous campaigns ending with the fall of Corinth, and he chafed under the inglorious restraint, longing for the release of his energies, the larger life of the soldier, the opportunity for distinction.

10

According to the text, why was Peyton Farquhar irritated?

(A) He was compelled to undertake a military obligation against his will.

(B) Despite his desire to join the army, he was made to remain behind.

(C) His affluence and achievements prevent him from pursuing his dream of secession.

(D) Above all, he longed to take part in a second military campaign at Corinth.

Section 1, Module 1: Reading and Writing

Directions ⌄

32:00
Hide

✎ Annotate   ⋮ More

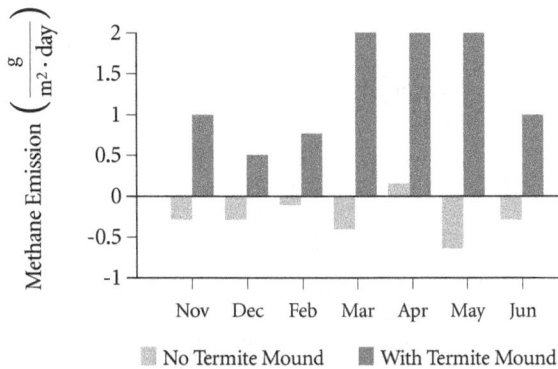

Methane Emission $\left(\frac{g}{m^2 \cdot day}\right)$

No Termite Mound   With Termite Mound

The findings from previous research suggest that termite mounds may play a considerable role in greenhouse gas emissions. Termites release substantial quantities of methane (CH_4) into the atmosphere as they digest plant matter. However, the precise extent of their impact on the overall greenhouse gas (GHG) balance is yet to be determined. A study by Helio Danilo Quevedo and colleagues assessed the effect of termite mounds on methane emissions by comparing emission levels near mounds to emission levels at control areas devoid of such mounds. The findings revealed that regions inhabited by termites produce significantly higher GHG emissions than regions without termite mounds.

11

Which choice best describes data from the graph that support the findings mentioned in the text?

- (A) In the presence of termite mounds, the methane emission was recorded at 1.9 g/m^2 per day in May, whereas in their absence, it was -0.7 g/m^2 per day.

- (B) The methane emission in the absence of termite mounds was -0.4 g/m^2 per day in March and -0.7 g/m^2 per day in May.

- (C) April is the only month during which areas without termite mounds exhibit a positive methane emission, while areas with termite mounds show a negative methane emission.

- (D) For a period of three months, the areas with termite mounds recorded a methane emission of approximately 2 g/m^2 per day.

Section 1, Module 1: Reading and Writing

Directions ∨

Annotate   More

Les Misérables is a French novel written by Victor Hugo first published in 1862. The novel tells the story of ex-convict Jean Valjean, who, after serving a nineteen-year prison sentence, breaks his parole and starts a new life. But before he breaks his parole the benevolent Bishop Myriel invites the ex-convict Jean Valjean to dine and lodge with him, inadvertently sparking Valjean's covetous thoughts toward the valuable silverware and utensils.The novel suggest that Valjean's labor during his incarceration did not earn him much, as in _____.

12

Which quotation from "*Les Misérables*" most effectively illustrates the claim?

- (A) "From the ladle one could get at least two hundred francs.—Double what he had earned in nineteen years."

- (B) "...with the mechanical persistence of revery, of a convict named Brevet, whom he had known in the galleys, and whose trousers had been upheld by a single suspender of knitted cotton."

- (C) "Those six sets of silver haunted him.—They were there.—A few paces distant."

- (D) "His mind wavered for a whole hour in fluctuations with which there was certainly mingled some struggle."

SCORE SHAKE

Back   Next

Section 1, Module 1: Reading and Writing

Directions ∨

Annotate   More

Recent studies indicate that creative pursuits, including art, music, and performance, can positively influence mental health. Research from the University of Westminster in London suggests that engaging in artistic activities like painting, playing musical instruments, and performing can decrease stress and anxiety while enhancing self-confidence and focus. The three-month study required participants to dedicate a minimum of two hours per week to creative endeavors. The findings highlight the value of allocating time for artistic activities to promote mental well-being.

13

Which statement, if true, would most likely weaken the study's implications?

- (A) After three months of involvement in artistic pursuits, participants experienced a considerable decrease in their stress levels.

- (B) Following a three-month engagement in artistic endeavors, participants noted an increased sense of confidence in their capabilities.

- (C) After participating in creative activities for three months, participants observed a substantial decline in their concentration levels.

- (D) Upon engaging in creative activities for three months, participants experienced a marked decrease in their anxiety levels.

SCORE SHAKE

Back   Next

Native American languages are diverse and unique, with over 500 different languages spoken by indigenous communities in North and South America. These languages have evolved over thousands of years and often have complex grammar structures and unique sounds. Many Native American languages are endangered, with fewer and fewer fluent speakers as younger generations shift towards more dominant languages. Efforts to preserve and revitalize Native American languages are ongoing. Many indigenous communities are working on teaching their languages to younger generations and incorporating the languages into schools and other educational programs. The preservation of these languages is crucial to maintaining cultural identity and promoting a deeper understanding of the rich history and diversity of indigenous peoples. Because of this, scholars in linguistics could generalize that _____

14

Which choice most logically completes the text?

(A) there is a notable link between acquiring languages and sustaining one's cultural identity.

(B) grasping the essence of a culture is often a vital precursor to mastering its language.

(C) the loss of indigenous Native American languages could have detrimental impacts on other cultures.

(D) learning more than one language is a highly effective method for preserving one's cultural identity.

Venturing into the depths of the Amazon rainforest, _____ teeming with diverse plant and animal species. This incredible biodiversity serves as a living testament to the wonders of nature, inspiring generations of scientists, conservationists, and nature enthusiasts alike.

15

Which choice completes the text so that it conforms to the conventions of Standard English?

(A) explorers find themselves immersed in a vibrant ecosystem

(B) immersion in the vibrant ecosystem is an awe-inspiring experience for explorers

(C) explorers' experience of being immersed in a vibrant ecosystem reveals the astonishing diversity

(D) vibrant ecosystems captivate explorers as they find themselves immersed in the rich biodiversity

Section 1, Module 1: Reading and Writing

Annotate   More

Directions ⌄

A fascinating and complex field, often perplexing the most brilliant _____ quantum physics continues to baffle even the brightest minds. Pioneers like Albert Einstein and Niels Bohr, pioneers in their time, contributed significantly to our understanding of the quantum world. Their groundbreaking work has laid the foundation for modern advancements in technology and scientific discovery.

16

Which choice completes the text so that it conforms to the conventions of Standard English?

- (A) thinkers
- (B) thinkers:
- (C) thinkers;
- (D) thinkers,

SCORE SHAKE

Back   Next

Section 1, Module 1: Reading and Writing

Annotate   More

Directions ⌄

Photography, a captivating art form, enables us to freeze moments in time and preserve memories. The first permanent photograph, which _____ in 1826, took an astounding eight hours of exposure. This lengthy process, during which the sun had to shine consistently, gave birth to a medium that now allows us to capture images in mere fractions of a second. Today, photography continues to evolve, consistently pushing the boundaries of creative expression.

17

Which choice completes the text so that it conforms to the conventions of Standard English?

- (A) are created by Joseph Nicéphore Niépce
- (B) have been created by Joseph Nicéphore Niépce
- (C) were created by Joseph Nicéphore Niépce
- (D) was created by Joseph Nicéphore Niépce

SCORE SHAKE

Back   Next

Semiconductors have revolutionized the way we live and communicate. Silicon, the most commonly used semiconductor material with excellent thermal conductivity and electron mobility, is transformed into silicon wafers through an intricate manufacturing process. These wafers are utilized in devices ranging from smartphones to solar panels, the very foundation of our digital _____ our technologically-driven world with each innovation.

18

Which choice completes the text so that it conforms to the conventions of Standard English?

- (A) age; shaping
- (B) age. Shaping
- (C) age shaping
- (D) age, shaping

Nestled in the heart of the mountains lies a quaint village known for its serene beauty and friendly locals. Surrounded by breathtaking landscapes, _____ bask in the warm glow of the setting sun. They often find themselves captivated by the harmonious blend of nature and tradition, experiencing tranquility that leaves a lasting impression long after they've departed.

19

Which choice completes the text so that it conforms to the conventions of Standard English?

- (A) the village offers a peaceful retreat for weary travelers, who
- (B) a peaceful retreat is offered by the village, that
- (C) the village's hospitality is a boon to weary travelers, who
- (D) the weariness of travelers is washed away by the village's peaceful retreat, that

A highly intelligent marine creature, the octopus thrives in various ocean habitats, including coral reefs and the ocean floor, and has an exceptional ability to change its color and texture that, despite its lack of bones, a defining characteristic of its class, _____ it to blend seamlessly with its surroundings.

20

Which choice completes the text so that it conforms to the conventions of Standard English?

- (A) enabling
- (B) to enable
- (C) to have enabled
- (D) enable

Gleaming beneath the desert sun, the mystifying Egyptian pyramids have intrigued historians and archaeologists for _____ in mystery, these ancient wonders boast an architectural complexity, illustrating the ingenuity of their creators. Despite relentless exploration and research, the pyramids' precise construction methods and purpose continue to elude scholars, sparking countless theories and debates that captivate the world's imagination.

21

Which choice completes the text so that it conforms to the conventions of Standard English?

- (A) millennia, shrouded
- (B) millennia. Shrouded
- (C) millennia shrouded
- (D) millennia and shrouded

Polar bears, known for their striking white fur, are expert swimmers and hunters in the Arctic. _____ their fur is actually translucent, appearing white due to light reflection, which aids in camouflaging them against icy landscapes. Moreover, these incredible animals are equipped with large paws and sharp claws, enabling them to maintain traction on ice and effectively capture prey.

22

Which choice completes the text with the most logical transition?

(A) By contrast,

(B) Likewise,

(C) Besides,

(D) In fact,

In 2013, celebrated Canadian author Alice Munro received the prestigious Nobel Prize in Literature for her exceptional mastery of the short story. _____ her works often delve into the intricacies of human relationships and the complexities of everyday life, capturing the depth and nuance of her characters through precise and evocative prose.

23

Which choice completes the text with the most logical transition?

(A) However,

(B) Moreover,

(C) As a result,

(D) Conversely,

Section 1, Module 1: Reading and Writing

Directions ⌄

32:00
Hide

✎ Annotate   ⋮ More

The transportation and delivery of goods across vast distances, once a slow and arduous process, were revolutionized by the emergence of logistics businesses. _____ these enterprises are undergoing a further transformation as technological advancements streamline processes and improve efficiency. Comparing past and present, logistics businesses must now adapt and innovate to satisfy the growing demands of customers and remain a vital component in the ever-evolving landscape of international trade.

24

Which choice completes the text with the most logical transition?

(A) Previously,

(B) For this reason,

(C) Currently,

(D) Instead,

SCORE SHAKE

Question 24 of 27 ⌃

Back   Next

Section 1, Module 1: Reading and Writing

Directions ⌄

32:00
Hide

✎ Annotate   ⋮ More

While researching a topic, a student has taken the following notes:

- Nanoneuroscience is a scientific field that incorporates both nanotechnology and neuroscience.
- Like all neuroscience, nanoneuroscience attempts to understand how the nervous system operates and how neurons organize in the brain.
- Nanotechnology is the study of the practical application of subatomic matter called nanoparticles.
- Nanoneuroscience investigates the use of nanoparticles in treating neurological problems such as Alzheimer's disease.

25

The student wants to emphasize a similarity between nanoneuroscience and nanotechnology. Which choice most effectively uses relevant information from the notes to accomplish this goal?

Ⓐ Nanoneuroscience and nanotechnology are both fields that study the use of nanoparticles.

Ⓑ Nanoneuroscience investigates the use of nanoparticles in treating neurological problems such as Alzheimer's disease and attempts to understand how the nervous system operates and how neurons organize in the brain.

Ⓒ Like all neuroscience, nanoneuroscience attempts to understand how the nervous system operates and how neurons organize in the brain; it investigates the use of nanoparticles in treating neurological problems such as Alzheimer's disease.

Ⓓ Nanotechnology, which is incorporated in nanoneuroscience, is the study of the practical application of subatomic matter, called nanoparticles.

While researching a topic, a student has taken the following notes:

- A praxinoscope uses a strip of pictures placed around the inner surface of a spinning cylinder to present a series of images that appear animated.
- Between 1892 and 1900, a projection praxinoscope was shown to more than 500,000 visitors at a museum in Paris.
- The images used in the device were hand-painted.
- Mirrors were used to project the images onto a screen.
- These animations were projected over a non-moving background scene and were accompanied by piano music, song, and some live dialogue.
- Some consider this the true beginning of film.

26

The student wants to explain the basic workings of a projection praxinoscope. Which choice most effectively uses relevant information from the notes to accomplish this goal?

(A) A projection praxinoscope, which uses mirrors to project images onto a screen, was shown to more than 500,000 visitors at a museum in Paris.

(B) A strip of pictures placed around the inner surface of a spinning cylinder is projected onto a screen using mirrors.

(C) Some consider the use of a projection praxinoscope to show animations between 1892 and 1900 at a museum in Paris to be the true beginning of film.

(D) The hand-painted images shown between 1892 and 1900 were projected over a non-moving background scene and were accompanied by piano music, song, and some live dialogue.

While researching a topic, a student has taken the following notes:

- Modern salvage operations, in which attempts are made to rescue a sunken ship and its cargo, began when practical diving helmets were invented in the 1830s.
- Using these helmets, divers were able to recover about two dozen cannons from a British gunship that sank in 1782.
- In 1839, a further salvage operation on the gunship involved breaking up the wreck with gunpowder before sending in divers.
- This operation was the first to feature the buddy system, in which divers always swam in pairs.
- Besides cannons and other weapons, medical instruments and silk clothing in good condition were recovered.

27

The student wants to emphasize what was new about the salvage operations on the British gunship. Which choice most effectively uses relevant information from the notes to accomplish this goal?

(A) The operations used the recently invented diving helmets and featured the buddy system.

(B) In addition to about two dozen cannons, medical instruments and silk clothing in good condition were recovered.

(C) Modern salvage operations such as those involving attempts to rescue the gunship and its cargo, began when practical diving helmets were invented in the 1830s.

(D) Divers were able to recover about two dozen cannons in 1782, and a further salvage operation on the gunship involved breaking up the wreck with gunpowder before sending in divers.

Practice Test Break

You can resume this practice test as soon as you're ready to move on. On test day, you'll wait until the clock counts down.

Take a Break

You may leave the room, but do not disturb students who are still testing.

Do not exit the app or close your device.

Testing won't resume until you return.

Follow these rules during the break:

1. Do not access your phone, smartwatch, textbooks, notes, or the internet.

2. Do not eat or drink in the test room.

3. Do not speak in the test room; outside the test room, do not discuss the exam with anyone.

Remaing Break Time:

9:52

Resume Testing

Section 1, Module 2: Reading and Writing

Directions ⌄

32:00
Hide

Annotate   More

Dr. Neil deGrasse Tyson, an astrophysicist and science communicator, has been a professor at several universities, including Princeton University and the City College of New York. He is known for his ability to explain complex scientific concepts in an engaging and _____ manner, using humor and pop culture references to make them relatable to a wider audience.

1

Which choice completes the text with the most logical and precise word or phrase?

(A) wary

(B) accessible

(C) prudent

(D) conventional

Section 1, Module 2: Reading and Writing

Directions ⌄

32:00
Hide

Annotate   More

In Daniel Defoe's renowned novel *"Robinson Crusoe,"* the protagonist, Robinson Crusoe, finds himself marooned on a desolate island where he must adapt to survive and create a life for himself. With no external assistance available, Crusoe faces the challenge of subsisting on the seemingly _____ island.

2

Which choice completes the text with the most logical and precise word or phrase?

(A) lurid

(B) sterile

(C) idyllic

(D) barren

Abraham Lincoln, the cherished American president, was renowned for his extraordinary oratory skills. The Gettysburg Address, in particular, stands out as an exemplary display of brevity and potency. Lincoln achieved this conciseness through _____ language and the deliberate use of a small number of impactful lines.

3

Which choice completes the text with the most logical and precise word or phrase?

(A) succinct

(B) extemporaneous

(C) colloquial

(D) literary

Many researchers have investigated the possible effects of climate change on diverse animal species. One scientist had postulated that increasing temperatures would result in a decrease in the population of a specific bird species. However, this hypothesis was ultimately _____ when new census data contradicted the initial findings. By employing meticulous data gathering and analysis, the researchers successfully presented evidence that countered the original assumption.

4

Which choice completes the text with the most logical and precise word or phrase?

(A) apprised

(B) corroborated

(C) debunked

(D) snubbed

Frankenstein, first published anonymously in 1818, was written by Mary Shelley. In this excerpt, the protagonist vehemently refuses to create another being like his first creation, despite being threatened with torture.

"I do refuse it," I replied; "and no torture shall ever extort a consent from me. You may render me the most miserable of men, but you shall never make me <u>base</u> in my own eyes. Shall I create another like yourself, whose joint wickedness might desolate the world? Begone! I have answered you; you may torture me, but I will never consent."

5

As used in the text, what does the word "base" most nearly mean?

- (A) immoral
- (B) ignorant
- (C) rudimentary
- (D) weak

In ideologically diverse societies, establishing shared moral and ethical principles is more challenging than it is in mono-cultural societies like those of Poland or Japan. In monocultures, people generally understand the social contract and expected code of conduct, which encompasses rules and meanings. Common cultural origins foster instantly comprehensible metaphors, symbols, and nonverbal behaviors. However, achieving conformity becomes difficult in demographically diverse societies or international settings, often referred to as multicultural individualistic societies. For example, the United States values individual effort and exhibits less concern for the group, making it a highly individualistic society.

6

Which choice best states the main idea of the text?

- (A) Finding shared moral and ethical values is more difficult in societies that have individualistic, diverse backgrounds.
- (B) The multicultural societies of nations like the United States tend to have competing ideologies.
- (C) Poland and Japan exemplify countries with shared cultural origins, which fosters easily comprehensible verbal and non-verbal communication.
- (D) It is difficult to move from a society that is monocultural to one that is high on individualism.

In March 2020, Jodi Pollack, co-worldwide head of Sotheby's 20th Century Design, made the tough decision to shift her mid-season sale online due to the COVID-19 pandemic. However, Pollack and her team had certain factors in their favor: the design market had been strong and growing for the past several seasons, and online they would have a captive audience who could be enticed with reasonable estimates. The sale's outcome surpassed expectations, achieving $4 million in profits and setting a record for online 20th-century design sales. A standout piece was a late nineteenth-century "Moorish" twisted-wire chandelier by Tiffany Studios that fetched $300,000—20 times its initial high estimate.

7

According to the text, what can be said about Sotheby's mid-season sale?

(A) It was, at the time, the most profitable design sale ever.

(B) It benefitted from factors that preceded the international COVID-19 pandemic.

(C) It exclusively featured items created in the 20th century.

(D) It was unusually profitable in large part because of the decision to make the company's estimates more reasonable.

The following text is from Henry Wadsworth Longfellow's 1863 poem "*Tales of a Wayside Inn*," a collection of poems in which Longfellow describes each of the occupants of an inn.

> Robert of Sicily, brother of Pope Urbane
> And Valmond, Emperor of Allemaine,
> Apparelled in magnificent attire,
> With retinue of many a knight and squire,
> On St. John's eve, at vespers, proudly sat
> And heard the priests chant the Magnificat,
> And as he listened, o'er and o'er again
> Repeated, like a burden or refrain,
> He caught the words, 'Deposuit potentes
> De sede, et exaltavit humiles;'
> And slowly lifting up his kingly head
> He to a learned clerk beside him said,
> 'What mean these words?' The clerk made answer meet,
> 'He has put down the mighty from their seat,
> And has exalted them of low degree.'
> Threat King Robert muttered scornfully,
> "T is well that such seditious words are sung
> Only by priests and in the Latin tongue;
> For unto priests and people be it known,
> There is no power can push me from my throne!'

8

Which is the main idea of the text?

(A) King Robert is bored by the repetitious chanting of the priests.

(B) King Robert is annoyed that the priests' words are spoken in a language he does not understand.

(C) King Robert believes that the priests are speaking words that are secretly meant to apply to him.

(D) King Robert is angered by the priests' words, which he states do not apply to him.

Filial duty demands that as parents grow old, their children should take care of them. This obligation increases as the children mature. As they gain wider perspectives and deeper insights, they are expected to embrace a greater sense of responsibility. Though the young are permitted to be innocent and unenlightened, they must ultimately accept their roles as caretakers of their aging parents. When my mother displays moments of vulnerability, I am transported to my own youth, and I am reminded of the lessons I learned as a child. Nevertheless, it could also be seen as a poignant indicator of her own aging and her transition to a new phase of life. It's a thought that I can't wrap my head around for the moment; a thought that I cannot fully embrace. <u>However, I know that while she grows, I grow too.</u>

9

Which choice best describes the function of the underlined sentence in the text as a whole?

(A) It shifts the focus of reflection from general maturity to the narrator's personal maturity.

(B) It highlights the similarity between the narrator and the mother regarding their response to the aging process.

(C) It laments the inevitable nature of the aging process and its impact on an individual's physical and mental well-being.

(D) It highlights the responsibility of children to care for their aging parents, even as the children themselves grow older.

Text 1
<u>Research has shown that individuals who have had early experiences with nature are more likely to engage in pro-environmental behaviors and support policies that protect the environment.</u> Thus, nature not only impacts individual development but also has a wider societal influence in shaping attitudes towards the environment and sustainability.

Text 2
Humans have a greater impact on shaping the environment than the environment has on shaping human behavior. Human activities have had a profound and lasting impact on Earth's ecosystems, leading to climate change, habitat destruction, and species extinction. While it is true that exposure to nature can instill an appreciation for the natural world, it is important to recognize that human actions are primarily influenced by cultural, societal, and economic factors. values, and belief systems, ultimately influencing our behavior throughout our lives.

10

Based on the texts, how would the author of Text 2 most likely respond to the underlined statement in Text 1?

(A) By pointing out that attitudes toward the environment are not primarily shaped by an individual's early exposure to nature

(B) By questioning the idea that experiencing nature directly leads to a deeper appreciation for the environment and its wonders

(C) By contrasting the extent to which nature influences individual human behavior with its influence on broader human society

(D) By commending people's inclination towards eco-friendly actions and endorsing environmentally conscious policies

The study of language, a quintessential aspect of the humanities, delves into the fascinating intricacies of human communication. As a multifaceted and evolving system, language enables us to convey emotions, thoughts, and abstract concepts, transcending the barriers of time and space. It is an essential tool that not only fosters connections between individuals and cultures but also serves as a mirror to our collective histories and experiences. By examining the nuances of linguistics, including syntax, semantics, and phonetics, researchers can uncover the roots of our shared human experience, offering insights into the complex tapestry of societies past and present. Language, an ever-changing and dynamic aspect of the humanities, embodies the essence of human ingenuity and adaptability.

11

According to the text, what can we discover from learning various aspects of a language?

(A) We learn that enhancing the expression of emotions, thoughts, and abstract ideas can foster human ingenuity and adaptability.

(B) We have the opportunity to explore common human emotions and encounters that unite us as a community.

(C) We realize that the diverse nuances of language stand as a testament to the barriers of time and space.

(D) We recognize the importance of language in communicating societal customs and manners essential for establishing a community.

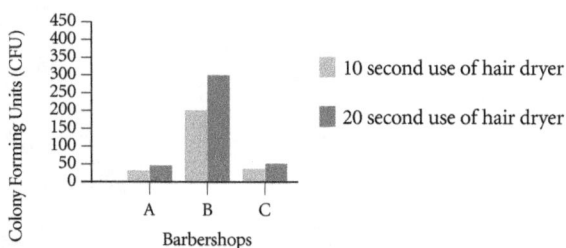

"Barbershops: a breeding ground for gossip and germs!" This witty saying reveals an overlooked truth about the potential public health risk in barbershops. One unsuspected culprit is the humble hair dryer, which can contribute to the spread of bacterial infections like *staphylococcus aureus*. Researcher Sulaiman A. Al Yousef investigated the bacterial contamination levels in hair dryers at three of these establishments. He collected air samples released by hair dryers after 10 and 20 seconds of use, culturing them on an agar medium. After 48 hours at 37°C, he counted the total number of bacteria present. Results showed significant contamination, with higher bacterial counts correlating to longer hair dryer use. For instance,

12

Which choice most effectively uses data from the graph to complete the example?

(A) in each sampled barbershop, the total bacterial count was greater when the hair dryers were operated for 20 seconds rather than for 10 seconds

(B) barbershop B exhibited a higher total bacterial count than the combined counts of both barbershop A and C

(C) in barbershop A, the bacterial count was higher for a 20-second use of the hair dryer compared to a 10-second use, whereas barbershop B displayed the opposite trend

(D) across all three barbershops, the total bacterial count was higher when the hair dryers were used for 10 seconds rather than for 20-seconds

Section 1, Module 2: Reading and Writing

Directions ∨

Annotate   More

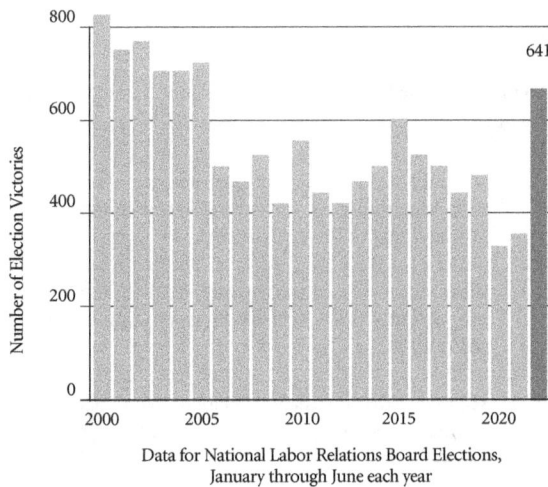

Data for National Labor Relations Board Elections,
January through June each year

Employees are coming together at some of America's most renowned businesses and in sectors once considered impervious to unionization. This is happening despite a long-term decrease in union membership, which has resulted in diminished benefits and wages that have failed to keep up with the cost of living. Recently, news reports have been filled with accounts of individuals ranging from baristas to warehouse workers voting in favor of unions and negotiating contracts, suggesting that unions may finally be experiencing a resurgence. In fact, a collection of recent data indicates that these union advancements are more than mere headlines. From election victories to collective efforts, 2022 has so far proven to be a successful year for unions. _____

13

Which choice best describes the function of the underlined sentence in the text as a whole?

(A) Since 2015, the election victories of pro-union candidates have consistently diminished.

(B) During the year 2022, unions triumphed in 641 elections—the highest number in almost two decades.

(C) From 2005 onward, election wins for candidates endorsing the Union have never reached the 600-mark.

(D) In the year 2000, the Union's robust support was evident through its unprecedented election successes with candidates who were pro-union.

Section 1, Module 2: Reading and Writing

Directions ∨

Annotate   More

The Moonlit Road is a 1907 short story by Ambrose Bierce. This story relates the tale of the murder of a character in the story, Julia Hetman, from the perspective of her son. In the story, the narrator implies that, as a boy, he did not fully recognize how badly he would suffer from his mother's death; _____.

14

Which quotation from "*The Moonlit Road*" most effectively illustrates the claim?

(A) "In the stress of privation and the need of effort I might sometimes forget the sombre secret ever baffling the conjecture that it compels"

(B) "Ah, that I might again dwell in that enchanted land! Unacquainted with grief, I knew not how to appraise my bereavement"

(C) "... with many other advantages usually valued by those having them and coveted by those who have them not I sometimes think that I should be less unhappy if they had been denied me"

(D) "I gave up my studies and remained with my father, who, naturally, was greatly changed. Always of a sedate, taciturn disposition, he now fell into so deep a dejection that nothing could hold his attention"

Effective learning hinges on the ability to engage students in the learning process. This engagement is paramount for ensuring that students remain motivated and receptive to new information. One crucial aspect of fostering this engagement is rapport-building, which cultivates trust, understanding, and respect between teacher and student. By nurturing this connection, educators create a positive learning environment that promotes open communication and active participation, without which _____.

15

Which choice most logically completes the text?

- (A) students will push themselves harder to compensate for the absence of understanding and communication

- (B) teachers' eagerness to connect with students will decline, resulting in a lackluster learning atmosphere

- (C) barriers to learning are minimized, allowing students to confidently explore and develop their skills

- (D) students may struggle to absorb and apply new concepts, leading to diminished academic performance

Great Expectation is the 1861 novel by Charles Dickens.

"It was interesting to be in the quiet old town once more, and it was not disagreeable to be here and there suddenly recognized and stared after. One or two of the tradespeople even darted out of their shops, and went a little way down the street before me, that they might turn, as if they had forgotten something, and pass me face to face—on which occasions I don't know whether they or I made the worse pretence; they of not doing it, or I of not seeing it. Still my position was a distinguished one, and I was not at all dissatisfied with it..." The text implies that the narrator felt _____.

16

Which choice most logically completes the text?

- (A) wary and powerless as a newcomer in town

- (B) indignant and confounded toward the residents of the town

- (C) uninterested and insignificant in a small old town

- (D) a sense of pride upon returning to his hometown

Section 1, Module 2: Reading and Writing

Directions ⌄

32:00
Hide

✎ Annotate   ⋮ More

Resembling a soft, elongated sack, the sea cucumber, *Holothuroidea Echinodermata*, plays a vital role in ocean ecosystems by breaking down _____ its odd appearance conceals a fascinating defense mechanism. When threatened, it expels its internal organs to deter predators, later regenerating these lost organs in a display of incredible resilience.

17

Which choice completes the text so that it conforms to the conventions of Standard English?

(A) detritus, however,

(B) detritus however,

(C) detritus, however;

(D) detritus; however,

SCORE SHΔKE

Question 17 of 27 ⌃

Back   Next

Section 1, Module 2: Reading and Writing

Directions ⌄

32:00
Hide

✎ Annotate   ⋮ More

The modern commerce landscape _____ by the introduction of the first credit card, created in 1950 by the founder of Diners Club International, Frank McNamara. The concept emerged from a forgotten wallet during a business dinner, sparking the idea of a card that deferred payment and paving the way for today's thriving credit industry.

18

Which choice completes the text so that it conforms to the conventions of Standard English?

(A) revolutionizes

(B) has been revolutionized

(C) will be revolutionized

(D) was revolutionized

SCORE SHΔKE

Question 18 of 27 ⌃

Back   Next

Triggered by the stock market crash of 1929, the Great Depression plunged millions into economic _____ endured years of struggle, the populace, both rich and poor, found themselves grappling with unemployment, poverty, and hunger, ultimately shaping a resilient generation that would forever remember the lessons learned during these trying times.

19

Which choice completes the text so that it conforms to the conventions of Standard English?

- (A) hardship and having
- (B) hardship. Having
- (C) hardship, having
- (D) hardship having

Beneath Antarctica's thick ice sheet lies the hidden gem of Lake Vostok, an enormous subglacial lake that remained undisturbed for millennia. Not until the 1990s _____ the lake's existence confirmed, sparking scientific interest in its potential to harbor life and offering insights into Earth's ancient climate.

20

Which choice completes the text so that it conforms to the conventions of Standard English?

- (A) was
- (B) were
- (C) have been
- (D) are

As an iconic air plant often associated with Southern Gothic imagery, Spanish moss thrives in humid, warm _____ gracefully from trees in the southeastern United States. Neither Spanish nor moss, this epiphyte belongs to the *Bromeliaceae* family and survives by absorbing nutrients and moisture from the air, contributing to the region's unique ambiance.

21

Which choice completes the text so that it conforms to the conventions of Standard English?

- (A) environments draping
- (B) environments. Draping
- (C) environments, draping
- (D) environments; draping

Numerous scientists, captivated by the spectacle, marvel at the elaborate mating rituals of bowerbirds, specifically the satin bowerbird. _____ "These captivating creatures, masters of seduction, construct intricate, decorative structures called bowers, using vibrant objects, tokens of their affection, to attract their mates—a testament to the artistry and complexity of nature's courtship displays."

22

Which choice completes the text so that it conforms to the conventions of Standard English?

- (A) An esteemed ornithologist, Dr. Jane Thompson observed with fascination,
- (B) An esteemed ornithologist Dr. Jane Thompson observed with fascination
- (C) An esteemed ornithologist Dr. Jane Thompson observed with fascination,
- (D) An esteemed ornithologist Dr. Jane Thompson, observed with fascination,

The digestive system of cows, specifically designed for processing fibrous plant material, consists of a complex, four-chambered stomach. Cows effectively break down cellulose-rich plants by regurgitating and thoroughly chewing their _____ re-swallowing partially digested food; and allowing microbes to ferment fibrous content.

23

Which choice completes the text so that it conforms to the conventions of Standard English?

- (A) cud, a bolus of partially digested food,
- (B) cud, a bolus of partially digested food;
- (C) cud; a bolus of partially digested food,
- (D) cud a bolus of partially digested food,

Milan Kundera's "*The Unbearable Lightness of Being*" probes into the intertwining lives of its characters, exploring the existential themes of love, freedom, and personal identity. _____ the novel skillfully intertwines political and philosophical undertones, reflecting the complexities of human existence during Czechoslovakia's Communist era.

24

Which choice completes the text with the most logical transition?

- (A) However,
- (B) For instance,
- (C) Likewise,
- (D) Thus,

The mysterious allure of abandoned places captivates urban explorers, who venture into these forgotten spaces to uncover their hidden stories. Decaying buildings, once bustling with life, now stand as silent witnesses to the passage of time. _____ these forsaken sites serve as poignant reminders of human transience and the ever-evolving nature of our built environment.

25

Which choice completes the text with the most logical transition?

- (A) Thus,
- (B) In contrast,
- (C) Similarly,
- (D) Still,

In 1903, the Wright brothers achieved the first powered, controlled, and sustained airplane flight, forever changing the landscape of human transportation. This groundbreaking invention sparked a race to innovate and advance aviation technology. _____ rapid advancements led to the evolution of commercial air travel, military aircraft, and space exploration, connecting the world like never before.

26

Which choice completes the text with the most logical transition?

- (A) Meanwhile,
- (B) Subsequently,
- (C) In summary,
- (D) Nonetheless,

While researching a topic, a student has taken the following notes:

- Basket weaving is a worldwide activity, but it is difficult to say when it started because the natural materials such as wood and grass used for basket weaving decay.
- Basket weaving was used in the Middle East prior to the use of pottery.
- Where no remains have been recovered, impressions found on surfaces suggest the use of baskets for storage.
- The most common impressions are imprints of the weave on clay pots.
- The oldest known baskets found in the Middle East were in upper Egypt.

27

The student wants to explain how evidence for early basket weaving has been established. Which choice most effectively uses relevant information from the notes to accomplish this goal?

(A) Basket weaving, a worldwide activity, was used in the Middle East prior to the use of pottery.

(B) Used in the Middle East prior to the use of pottery, the natural materials such as wood and grass used for basket weaving decay.

(C) Impressions such as the imprints of the weave on clay pots suggest the use of baskets for storage.

(D) It is difficult to say when basket weaving started because the natural materials such as wood and grass used for basket weaving decay.

TEST 1 Module 1		
No.	Answer	Question Type
1	D	Text Completion
2	B	Text Completion
3	D	Text Completion
4	A	Text Completion
5	B	Vocabulary in Context
6	C	Function
7	B	Main Purpose
8	A	Main Purpose / Poem
9	C	Cross-Text
10	B	Direct Comprehension / Literature
11	A	Command of Evidence / Quantitative
12	A	Command of Evidence / Literature
13	C	Command of Evidence / Textual
14	A	Inference
15	A	Conventions of Standard English
16	D	Conventions of Standard English
17	D	Conventions of Standard English
18	D	Conventions of Standard English
19	A	Conventions of Standard English
20	D	Conventions of Standard English
21	B	Conventions of Standard English
22	D	Transition
23	B	Transition
24	C	Transition
25	A	Note Summary
26	B	Note Summary
27	A	Note Summary

TEST 1 Module 2		
No.	Answer	Question Type
1	B	Text Completion
2	D	Text Completion
3	A	Text Completion
4	C	Text Completion
5	A	Vocabulary in Context
6	A	Main Idea
7	B	Direct Comprehension
8	D	Main Idea / Poem
9	A	Function
10	A	Cross-Text
11	B	Direct Comprehension
12	A	Command of Evidence / Quantitative
13	B	Command of Evidence / Quantitative
14	B	Command of Evidence / Literature
15	D	Inference
16	D	Inference
17	D	Conventions of Standard English
18	D	Conventions of Standard English
19	B	Conventions of Standard English
20	A	Conventions of Standard English
21	C	Conventions of Standard English
22	C	Conventions of Standard English
23	B	Conventions of Standard English
24	C	Transition
25	A	Transition
26	B	Transition
27	C	Note Summary

DIGITAL SAT Advanced SCORING CHART
Raw score to Score Conversion Chart

Raw Score	Score	Incorrect	Score
54	800	26	530
53	770	25	530
52	740	24	510
51	730	23	510
50	710	22	490
49	710	21	480
48	690	20	480
47	680	19	460
46	680	18	450
45	670	17	430
44	660	16	400
43	650	15	380
42	630	14	360
41	630	13	340
40	620	12	330
39	620	11	310
38	620	10	300
37	610	9	280
36	600	8	260
35	600	7	260
34	590	6	250
33	590	5	240
32	580	4	220
31	580	3	200
30	570	2	200
29	560	1	200
28	550	0	200
27	540		

Digital SAT
Practice Test #III

The questions in this section address a number of important reading and writing skills. Each question includes one or more passages, which may include a table or graph. Read each passage and question carefully, and then choose the best answer to the question based on the text(s).

All questions in this section are multiple-choice with four answer choices. Each question has a single best answer.

Section 1, Module 1: Reading and Writing

Directions ∨

32:00
Hide

Annotate   More

Seasonal shifts bring changes in weather patterns and environmental conditions, so it's vital for governing bodies to share relevant information with the public to promote safety and environmental conservation. Each year, during spring, the Forest Service issues a warning about the heightened risk of forest fires and urges people to exercise _____ caution in wooded areas. By following these recommendations, individuals can help reduce wildfires.

1

Which choice completes the text with the most logical and precise word or phrase?

- (A) sedentary
- (B) novel
- (C) moderate
- (D) extreme

SCORE SHAKE

Question 1 of 27 ∧

Next

Section 1, Module 1: Reading and Writing

Directions ∨

32:00
Hide

Annotate   More

The work of Max Weber, a pioneer in the field of sociology, was _____ by a student who aided in collecting and organizing a plethora of data. This collaboration ultimately contributed to the development of Weber's groundbreaking ideas on social stratification, power, and authority.

2

Which choice completes the text with the most logical and precise word or phrase?

- (A) prevented
- (B) facilitated
- (C) limited
- (D) compromised

SCORE SHAKE

Question 2 of 27 ∧

Back   Next

Section 1, Module 1: Reading and Writing

Directions ∨

32:00
Hide

Annotate   More

A price on carbon can be implemented via cap-and-trade programs, which limit the total quantity of emissions per year. This _____ is enforced using tradable emissions permits that any emissions source must own to cover its emissions. The market for buying and selling these allowances creates the carbon price.

3

Which choice completes the text with the most logical and precise word or phrase?

(A) diminution

(B) constraint

(C) application

(D) resolution

SCORE SHAKE

Back   Next

Section 1, Module 1: Reading and Writing

Directions ∨

32:00
Hide

Annotate   More

Sir Edmund Hillary encountered numerous challenges during his mountaineering career, one of which occurred during his famous climb of Mount Everest in 1953 when he and Tenzing Norgay found themselves stranded on a narrow ridge of rock. In this precarious situation, Sir Edmund Hillary demonstrated his _____ footwork skills, which enabled him to extricate himself and safely continue the climb.

4

Which choice completes the text with the most logical and precise word or phrase?

(A) lucrative

(B) disingenuous

(C) adroit

(D) capricious

SCORE SHAKE

Back   Next

Section 1, Module 1: Reading and Writing

Directions ⌄

32:00
Hide

✎ Annotate   ⋮ More

The origin of the internet is firmly rooted in the circumstances of the Cold War, a period during which nuclear conflict <u>featured</u> as potentially the most immediate and catastrophic of all global dangers. The launch of Sputnik 1 on October 4th, 1957, by the Soviet Union, spawned a very specific fear: if nations were capable of launching space satellites, they might also be capable of launching long-distance nuclear attacks.

5

As used in the text, what does the word "featured" most nearly mean?

(A) appeared

(B) described

(C) participated

(D) erupted

SCORE SHΛKE

Question 5 of 27 ⌃

Back   Next

Section 1, Module 1: Reading and Writing

Directions ⌄

32:00
Hide

✎ Annotate   ⋮ More

The following text is from R.C. Lehmann's poem "*The Lean-To-Shed*," published in 1918. The speaker is a child. The Lean-To-Shed refers to a simple and practical type of outdoor storage structure that gardeners store their tools.

I've a palace set in a garden fair,
    And, oh, but the flowers are rich and rare,

    And whenever I go there, early or late,
    The two tame dragons who guard the gate

      Get up with a grin
      And let me in.

    Then I pour them drink out of golden flagons,
    Drink for my two tame trusty dragons...
      But John,
      Who's a terrible fellow for chattering on,
      John declares
      They are Teddy-bears;
    And the palace itself, he has often said,
    Is only the gardener's lean-to-shed.

6

Which choice best states the main purpose of the text?

(A) To show that the child has not fooled John

(B) To express the longing the child has for an imaginary place

(C) To provide details about the environment in which the child lives

(D) To convey the rich imagination of the speaker

SCORE SHΛKE

Question 6 of 27 ⌃

Back   Next

Bridging the gap between health and longevity, universal healthcare coverage emerges as a catalyst for enhanced well-being and a longer life span. Synthetic control methods, which have gained popularity in recent years, enable the comparison of health outcomes across countries with different welfare state policies. Research from Harvard Kennedy School reveals that countries with universal healthcare coverage experience better health outcomes than those without. Additionally, a study by the University of California, Berkeley, found that countries with universal healthcare coverage have an average life expectancy nearly three years longer than countries lacking such coverage.

7

Which choice best states the main idea of the text?

(A) Measuring life expectancy serves as an effective means to gauge the success of universal healthcare coverage.

(B) The analysis of health outcomes was conducted to examine the influence of universal healthcare coverage.

(C) Universal healthcare coverage is effective in elevating health and wellbeing while extending life expectancy.

(D) Utilizing synthetic control methods, researchers evaluated the implications of welfare state policies.

A pioneering figure in the world of ethnographic fieldwork emerged in the form of Bronisław Malinowski, who made a lasting impact on the discipline of anthropology. He introduced the groundbreaking concept of "participant observation," which marked a paradigm shift in research methodology. By encouraging researchers to fully immerse themselves in the cultures they were investigating, Malinowski fostered a more profound and genuine understanding of human societies. His legacy continues to resonate in modern ethnography, and his contributions are celebrated for their enduring influence on the study of diverse cultures.

8

Which choice best states the main purpose of the text?

(A) To explore how Malinowski devised an innovative research methodology

(B) To explain the "participant observation" approach and its influence on the discipline of anthropology

(C) To highlight Malinowski's significant impact on the discipline of anthropology

(D) To compare Malinowski's approach to methodologies employed in contemporary ethnography

Text 1

Advocates for animal research assert that animal studies can yield significant findings applicable to humans. Despite notable distinctions in the way humans and animals behave and interact socially, evidence from animal studies frequently justifies subsequent research in human subjects, enabling researchers to pinpoint potential risks and side effects of treatments or interventions. This knowledge ultimately contributes to the refinement of clinical trials and the enhancement of patient safety.

Text 2

The idea that animal research is applicable to humans is highly controversial. Many critics argue that <u>animal studies may not adequately replicate the complexity of human behaviors and social interactions</u>, making it difficult to generalize findings to human psychology and behavior.

9

Based on the texts, how would the author of Text 1 most likely respond to the underlined statement in Text 2?

- (A) By stating that animal research remains a vital tool to justify further studies and identify potential risks, despite its limitations

- (B) By underscoring the intricacy of human behavior and interpersonal dynamics, which may not be wholly mirrored in animal research

- (C) By maintaining the position that significant advancements in scientific research are contingent only upon the effective use of animal studies

- (D) By suggesting that the improvement of clinical trials and the enhancement of patient safety can lead to more efficient and reliable outcomes in animal research

It's fascinating and somewhat surprising that the average person sheds around 40 pounds of skin throughout his or her lifetime. This substantial loss results from the body's continuous renewing and regenerating its outermost layer, the epidermis. Our skin is constantly shedding dead cells and producing new ones to replace them in a process called desquamation. In fact, we shed around 30,000 to 40,000 dead skin cells per minute. This natural process helps maintain a protective barrier against external factors like bacteria, viruses, and environmental irritants. Additionally, shedding dead skin cells aids in maintaining the skin's overall health, appearance, and texture. The accumulation of all these shed cells over a lifetime amounts to that staggering 40 pounds, a testament to the body's amazing regenerative capabilities.

10

According to the text, which of the following statements about the process of desquamation is NOT supported by the text?

- (A) Desquamation involves the shedding and subsequent replacement of dead skin cells.

- (B) Shedding dead skin cells contributes to maintaining a protective barrier against outside elements.

- (C) Due to desquamation, an individual typically sheds around 40 pounds of skin throughout his or her life.

- (D) Desquamation serves as the body's reaction to counteract the detrimental impact of sunlight on the skin.

Arctic Sea Ice Minimum Area

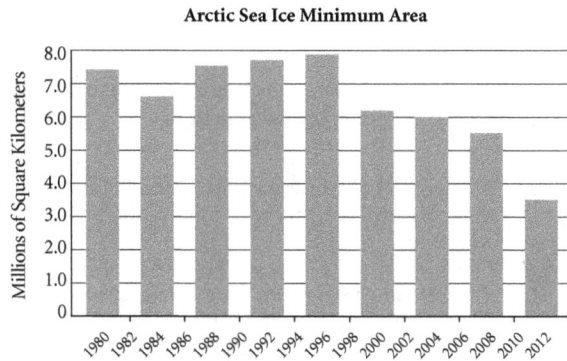

Arctic ice melting because of climate change is an alarming issue, causing reduced polar wildlife habitats, rising sea levels, and disrupted indigenous livelihoods. This phenomenon affects global ecosystems, economies, and communities. Peter Wadhams, a leading expert in Arctic sea ice and head of the Polar Ocean Physics Group at the University of Cambridge, is concerned about the rapid decline of Arctic sea ice and its impact on the climate. He believes the loss of sea ice contributes to global warming through a feedback loop: as the ice melts, exposed ocean surfaces absorb more sunlight, leading to further warming and ice loss. Wadhams emphasizes that Arctic ice will continue to melt if global carbon emissions aren't significantly reduced.

11

Which choice best describes data from the graph that support the argument made by Wadhams?

- (A) The pattern indicates that the quantity of ice could potentially plummet to zero in just a few years.

- (B) The trend exhibits a pronounced and discernible decrease since 2000.

- (C) The data reveals a reduction of 3 million square kilometers of ice between 1980 and 1990.

- (D) The data demonstrate a steady decline in Arctic ice from 1984 through 1988.

Section 1, Module 1: Reading and Writing

Directions ⌄

32:00
Hide

✎
Annotate

⋮
More

GDP as a Share of World GDP

1st
Opium War:
1839-1842

2nd
Opium War:
1856-1860

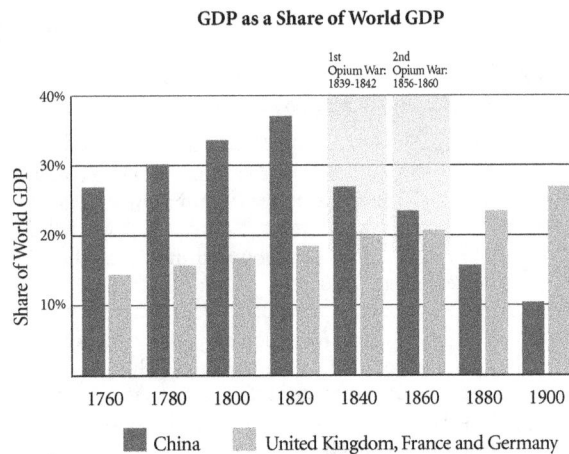

China   United Kingdom, France and Germany

Following the Opium Wars in the mid-19th century, China's share of global GDP experienced a dramatic decline. Prior to these conflicts, China held a significant portion of the world's economic output, with its vast population, rich natural resources, and advanced agricultural practices. However, the devastating impact of the Opium Wars, including the forced opening of Chinese ports to foreign trade, led to economic instability and decline. The country's once-thriving industries suffered heavily as foreign imports flooded the market, particularly in textiles and agriculture. This period of turmoil, combined with internal strife and political upheaval, contributed to China's diminished role in the global economy, with its share of world GDP dropping considerably from its pre-Opium Wars position.

12

Which choice best describes data from the graph that support the information discussed in the text?

(A) During the 18th and early 19th centuries, China's share of global GDP surpassed that of the United Kingdom.

(B) By 1880, China still maintained a larger share of global GDP than any European nation.

(C) China's share of global GDP dropped from 35% before the Opium Wars to nearly 10% following the conflicts.

(D) Following the Opium Wars, the United Kingdom started to assert dominance in the global economy, surpassing France and Germany.

Many economic researchers have been intrigued by the possible effects of providing individuals with a universal basic income (UBI). Those who have explored the topic frequently propose that implementing a universal basic Income policy would may considerably lower poverty rates and reduce economic disparities in society. In a recent study at the University of Washington, researchers focused on a rural community characterized by high poverty and income inequality. They randomly assigned 500 residents to receive a monthly $1,000 UBI (treatment group) or no extra support (control group) for 18 months. Socioeconomic and employment data were collected before and after the trial to assess the effectiveness of UBI in alleviating poverty and diminishing income inequality within the community.

13

Which finding, if true, would most strongly support the researchers' proposal?

- (A) The treatment group exhibited a notable increase in job opportunities, higher workforce participation, and improved job quality compared to the control group.

- (B) The treatment group displayed a higher rate of unemployment and lower participation in the workforce.

- (C) The treatment group demonstrated a lower unemployment rate at the cost of accepting lower-paying, lower-quality jobs than did the control group, who had higher-paying and more fulfilling jobs.

- (D) The treatment group exhibited a heightened sense of security and satisfaction that could not be quantified by the employment data, in contrast to the control group.

Section 1, Module 1: Reading and Writing

32:00
Hide

Directions ∨

Annotate   More

The flipped classroom model, in which students learn content online at home and complete homework in class under teacher guidance, represents a departure from conventional education. Traditional teaching, characterized by teacher-centered learning, often involves students passively absorbing information through lectures and demonstrations, with the educator serving as the primary source of knowledge. Flipped learning differs from traditional teaching by allowing learners to explore content independently at home and apply their knowledge through collaborative classroom activities and problem-solving. _____

14

Which choice most logically completes the text?

(A) Flipped learning underscores elements of teacher-centered learning through the use of online lessons crafted by educators, ensuring their guidance remains integral to the process.

(B) By reversing the conventional classroom structure, the flipped model empowers students to take charge of their education, leading to a more student-centered learning experience.

(C) In both traditional classroom settings and flipped learning structures, the significance of teachers in students' education continues to grow increasingly vital.

(D) Improved student performance in flipped learning demonstrates that teacher-centered learning environments can facilitate active information absorption by students.

Modular homes have revolutionized the housing industry with their innovative design and efficient construction process. _____ customizable nature allows for personalized living spaces tailored to individual needs, making them a popular choice for modern homebuyers. These eco-friendly, affordable options redefine the concept of comfortable living.

15

Which choice completes the text so that it conforms to the conventions of Standard English?

- (A) They're
- (B) Their
- (C) It's
- (D) Its

The fluorescent light bulb, a remarkable invention, once transformed the world of lighting with its energy-saving capabilities. Emitting a soft glow, it illuminates spaces _____ creating a cozy ambiance. This long-lasting, cost-effective solution has been widely adopted in homes and workplaces alike.

16

Which choice completes the text so that it conforms to the conventions of Standard English?

- (A) between, and beneath objects,
- (B) between and beneath objects,
- (C) between and beneath, objects,
- (D) between, and beneath objects

A groundbreaking study on American crime rates, conducted _____ revealed significant correlations between socioeconomic factors and criminal activity. Their findings emphasize the need for targeted interventions to reduce crime and improve community safety nationwide.

17

Which choice completes the text so that it conforms to the conventions of Standard English?

(A) by researchers Dr. Jennifer Thompson and Dr. Michael Johnson,

(B) by researchers Dr. Jennifer Thompson, and Dr. Michael Johnson,

(C) by researchers, Dr. Jennifer Thompson and Dr. Michael Johnson,

(D) by researchers, Dr. Jennifer Thompson and Dr. Michael Johnson

SCORE SHAKE

Back   Next

Pioneering research in material science, led by Dr. Alice Chen and Dr. David Kim, explores the development of advanced _____ these materials exhibit extraordinary properties with potential applications in various industries. Their work holds great promise for revolutionizing fields such as electronics, energy, and healthcare.

18

Which choice completes the text so that it conforms to the conventions of Standard English?

(A) nanomaterials,

(B) nanomaterials, also

(C) nanomaterials;

(D) nanomaterials also,

SCORE SHAKE

Back   Next

Section 1, Module 1: Reading and Writing
Directions ⌄

32:00
Hide

✎ Annotate   ⋮ More

In biophysics, scholars have made significant strides in understanding protein folding mechanisms. By studying the complex interplay of forces, _____ potentially leading to groundbreaking medical advancements.

19

Which choice completes the text so that it conforms to the conventions of Standard English?

- (A) scientists' aim is to illuminate the relationship between molecular structure and function,
- (B) the relationship between molecular structure and function is at the heart of scientists' aim,
- (C) the aim of scientists is to shed light on the relationship between molecular structure and function,
- (D) scientists aim to shed light on the relationship between molecular structure and function,

Research on the anthropology of sports, led by Dr. Emily Smith and Dr. Carlos Garcia, examines the sociocultural aspects of athletic activities. Their work encompasses the study of rituals in ancient sports, often steeped in religious _____ a crucial aspect of individual and group dynamics; and the impact of globalization on sports culture, an ever-evolving phenomenon shaped by social and economic forces.

20

Which choice completes the text so that it conforms to the conventions of Standard English?

- (A) significance; the role of sports in identity formation;
- (B) significance; the role of sports in identity formation,
- (C) significance, the role of sports in identity formation,
- (D) significance, the role of sports in identity formation;

Traditionally crafted by the skilled hands of the Navajo people in the American Southwest, hand-woven textiles hold a special place in the realm of textile arts, reflecting a unique and deeply rooted artistic _____ intricate designs inspired by ancestral motifs, rich symbolism embedded in cultural narratives, and vibrant colors drawn from the natural landscape.

21

Which choice completes the text so that it conforms to the conventions of Standard English?

(A) legacy:

(B) legacy;

(C) legacy

(D) legacy.

Traveling offers us the opportunity to experience new environments, meet different people, and learn about diverse customs. _____ it challenges us to step out of our comfort zones, promoting personal growth and resilience. By embracing these adventures, we can gain a deeper appreciation for the rich tapestry of human experiences around the world.

22

Which choice completes the text with the most logical transition?

(A) Additionally,

(B) As a result,

(C) However,

(D) For example,

Exploring diverse cultures enriches our understanding of humanity, broadening our perspectives and fostering empathy for others. It allows us to appreciate the unique customs, traditions, and values that shape our world. _____ by embracing cultural diversity, we can create a more inclusive and harmonious global community.

23

Which choice completes the text with the most logical transition?

(A) However,

(B) Therefore,

(C) Meanwhile,

(D) Similarly,

While researching a topic, a student has taken the following notes:

- A singularity is a condition in which the intensity of gravity causes spacetime to break down.
- It has no location or duration.
- The initial singularity is a singularity that some believe existed before the Big Bang at the formation of the universe.
- The earliest period of time in the universe, immediately after the initial singularity, is known as the Planck epoch, a period of very high energy.
- Because of that energy, the theory of general relativity alone seems unable to predict what happened during the epoch.
- An alternate, string-theory model of the early universe takes that environment into account.

24

The student wants to summarize the reason for an alternate model of the universe. Which choice most effectively uses relevant information from the notes to accomplish this goal?

(A) The theory of general relativity alone, because of the high energy environment during the Planck Epoch, seems unable to predict what happened during this time.

(B) The initial singularity is a condition in which the intensity of gravity causes spacetime to break down.

(C) The string-theory model of the early universe takes the high energy of the Planck epoch into account.

(D) The initial singularity that some believe existed before the Big Bang at the formation of the universe has no location or duration.

While researching a topic, a student has taken the following notes:

- Solar panels installed on residential roofs can reduce how much the residents pay for their daily energy needs.
- The location and slope of the roofs can be obstacles to their effectiveness.
- A system was devised that varies the angle of the panels to keep them perpendicular to the Sun.
- A significant number of residents objected to the appearance of the system.
- At the request of the residents, a design study was conducted.
- The study investigated ways to meet the objective of the system while minimizing this protest.

25

The student wants to present the aim of the design study. Which choice most effectively uses relevant information from the notes to accomplish this goal?

(A) The location and slope of the residential roofs on which solar panels have been installed to reduce how much the residents pay for their daily energy needs can be obstacles to the panels' effectiveness.

(B) The study to meet the system's objective was conducted at the request of the residents of the houses on which the panels were installed.

(C) A significant number of residents objected to the appearance of a system that keeps the angle of solar panels—installed on the residents' roofs to reduce how much they pay for their daily energy—perpendicular to the Sun.

(D) How to keep in place a system that varies the angle of the solar panels to keep them perpendicular to the Sun while minimizing objections to the appearance of the system was investigated.

While researching a topic, a student has taken the following notes:

- A "field holler" is a type of work song sung solo or as call-and-response by field slaves in the United States.
- Field hollers had origins in the music of West Africa, from which most of the first slaves originated.
- Like work songs, which were sung in groups, hollers were sometimes used to communicate thoughts and feelings the slaves couldn't otherwise express safely.
- A significant percentage of the slaves were Islamic, and the style of singing used in field hollers is possibly related to Islamic music.
- Field hollers and work songs eventually influenced gospel music, the blues, and other musical styles whose practitioners were predominantly African-American.

26

The student wants to emphasize the difference between field hollers and work songs. Which choice most effectively uses relevant information from the notes to accomplish this goal?

(A) Field hollers had origins in the music of West Africa, and the style of singing is possibly related to Islamic music, as a significant percentage of the salves were Islamic.

(B) Field hollers, which had origins in the music of West Africa, from which most of the first slaves originated, eventually influenced gospel music, the blues, and other musical styles whose practitioners were predominantly African-American.

(C) Work songs were sung by a group, and field hollers were sung solo or as call-and-response.

(D) Work songs, which were sung in groups, eventually influenced gospel music, the blues, and other musical styles whose practitioners were predominantly African-American.

Section 3, Module 1: Reading and Writing

Directions ⌄

32:00
Hide

✎ Annotate   ⋮ More

While researching a topic, a student has taken the following notes:

- The Bauhaus was a German art school that combined fine arts with crafts.
- The school became known for its focus on unifying artistry with function.
- The founder, architect Walter Gropius, was guided by a vision of bringing all the arts together.
- Simple geometric shapes without elaborate decorations are typical of the Bauhaus style taught at the school.
- It was highly influential on architecture, design, and typography.
- The Nazi movement of the time criticized the Bauhaus style as being "un-German."

27

The student wants to introduce the Bauhaus to an audience unfamiliar with the school. Which choice most effectively uses relevant information from the notes to accomplish this goal?

(A) Simple geometric shapes without elaborate decorations are typical of the style produced by the Bauhaus, which was founded by the school's founder, the architect Walter Gropius.

(B) A German art school that combined fine arts with crafts and focused on unifying artistry with function, the Bauhaus was highly influential on architecture, design, and typography

(C) The Bauhaus style that was taught at the German art school was criticized at the time by the Nazi party as being "un-German."

(D) An architect and founder, Walter Gropius, who established the Bauhaus, a German art school that combined fine arts with crafts, was guided by a vision of bringing all the arts together.

Practice Test Break

You can resume this practice test as soon as you're ready to move on. On test day, you'll wait until the clock counts down.

Take a Break

You may leave the room, but do not disturb students who are still testing.

Do not exit the app or close your device.

Testing won't resume until you return.

Follow these rules during the break:

1. Do not access your phone, smartwatch, textbooks, notes, or the internet.

2. Do not eat or drink in the test room.

3. Do not speak in the test room; outside the test room, do not discuss the exam with anyone.

Remaing Break Time:

9:52

Resume Testing

It is not uncommon for members of the clergy to conclude a public speaking engagement with _____. These closing blessings often invoke divine protection or guidance for the gathered community.

1

Which choice completes the text with the most logical and precise word or phrase?

- (A) a critique
- (B) an imprecation
- (C) a fable
- (D) a benediction

As the Spanish Civil War progressed, it became increasingly marked by foreign interventions and shifting alliances, making for _____ situation that belied the war's straightforward beginnings. The involvement of powers such as Nazi Germany and the Soviet Union further complicated the conflict, transforming it into a proxy battle of competing ideologies.

2

Which choice completes the text with the most logical and precise word or phrase?

- (A) a convoluted
- (B) an irrelevant
- (C) a deplored
- (D) a retrenched

Despite Adele's apparently _____ demeanor during her concerts, she has been candid about the overwhelming stage fright and anxiety she experiences before performing in front of an audience. Her struggles with these issues have led her to cancel shows and even experience physical symptoms such as vomiting. Nevertheless, Adele has also acknowledged the therapeutic power of performing and the joy she gets from connecting with her fans through her music.

3

Which choice completes the text with the most logical and precise word or phrase?

- (A) eminent
- (B) placid
- (C) ecstatic
- (D) tumultuous

Back   Next

In 1977, in a remarkable and bold display of diplomatic courage, President Anwar el-Sadat of Egypt, disregarding _____ criticism in the Arab world and in his own government, formally accepted Prime Minister Menachem Begin's invitation to visit Israel to address Israel's parliament. This historic event marked the first time an Arab leader had set foot on Israeli soil and laid the groundwork for the eventual signing of the Camp David Accords.

4

Which choice completes the text with the most logical and precise word or phrase?

- (A) scathing
- (B) blemished
- (C) circumstantial
- (D) malignant

Back   Next

Section 1, Module 2: Reading and Writing

Directions ∨

32:00
Hide

Annotate   More

The Cask of Amontillado is a short story by the American writer Edgar Allan Poe, first published in the November 1846 issue of *Godey's Lady's Book*.

"Let us go, nevertheless. The cold is merely nothing. Amontillado! You have been imposed upon. And as for Luchresi, he cannot distinguish Sherry from Amontillado."
    Thus speaking, Fortunato possessed himself of my arm; and putting on a mask of black silk and drawing a roquelaure closely about my person, I <u>suffered</u> him to hurry me to my palazzo.

5

As used in the text, what does the word "suffered" most nearly mean?

(A) distressed

(B) allowed

(C) watched

(D) urged

Section 1, Module 2: Reading and Writing

Directions ∨

32:00
Hide

Annotate   More

The following text is from the 1921 poem "*The Snow Man*" by Wallace Stevens.

One must have a mind of winter
To regard the frost and the boughs
Of the pine-trees crusted with snow;

And have been cold a long time
To behold the junipers shagged with ice,
The spruces rough in the distant glitter

Of the January sun; and not to think
Of any misery in the sound of the wind,
In the sound of a few leaves,
…
For the listener, who listens in the snow,
And, nothing himself, beholds
Nothing that is not there and the nothing that is.

6

Which choice best states the main purpose of the text?

(A) To lament the unforgiving and frigid nature of the winter season often accompanied by harsh winds.

(B) To appreciate the captivating beauty and delightful sensory experiences provided by the natural world during the winter season.

(C) To emphasize the value of detaching from personal emotions and biases to experience and appreciate the world.

(D) To highlight the significance of attentive listening in order to genuinely cherish the beauty of the natural world.

The Gift of the Magi, is a short story by O. Henry first published in 1905. The story takes place in a modest apartment where the two main characters, Della and Jim, a young married couple, live. They are struggling financially, which is evident from their humble surroundings

　　There was a pier-glass between the windows of the room. Perhaps you have seen a pier-glass in an $8 flat. <u>A very thin and very agile person may, by observing his reflection in a rapid sequence of longitudinal strips, obtain a fairly accurate conception of his looks.</u> Della, being slender, had mastered the art, though she would gladly trade that skillset for a vanity mirror with gilded edges, intricate carvings, and set against a backdrop of opulent wallpaper.

7

Which choice best describes the function of the underlined sentence in the text as a whole?

(A) It is employed to underscore the unattractiveness of the apartment.

(B) It is used to emphasize how little money the couple has.

(C) It serves to illustrate how slender Della is.

(D) It shows Della's ability to do the most she can with what she has.

The following text is from American poet Ella Wheeler Wilcox's poem "*The Law.*" A "thrush" is a type of bird.

　　The tide of love swells in me with such force,
　　　　It sweeps away all hate and all distrust.
　　As eddying straws and particles of dust
　　　　Are lost by some swift river in its course.

　　So much I love my friends, my life, my art,
　　　　Each shadow flies; the light dispels the gloom.
　　Love is so fair, I find I have no room
　　　　For anything less worthy in my heart.

　　Love is a germ which we can cultivate -
　　　　To grace and perfume sweeter than the rose,
　　Or leave neglected while our heart soil grows
　　　　Rank with that vile and poison thistle, hate.

　　Love is a joyous thrush, that one can teach
　　　　To sing sweet lute-like songs which all may hear.
　　Or we can silence him and tune the ear
　　　　To caw of crows, or to the vulture's screech

8

Which choice best describes the overall structure of the text?

(A) A theme is stated and supporting examples are given and objections addressed.

(B) A personal declaration is made in the first stanza, and generalizations are developed to show the universality of the idea in the remainder of the poem.

(C) The first two stanzas develop a viewpoint, while the second two stanzas alternate between this theme and a warning against opposing this view.

(D) Each stanza other than the first provides examples of the general theme presented in the first stanza.

Text 1

The over-prescription of medication for mental health disorders has led some individuals in the field to recommend an increase in non-pharmacological treatments. Supporters of this position argue that medication is frequently perceived as a quick solution for mental health challenges, potentially leading to adverse side effects without addressing core issues. They endorse the use of non-pharmacological strategies—including therapy, lifestyle changes, and alternative treatments—as primary interventions.

Text 2

Medication plays an essential role in addressing mental health disorders and must not be disregarded. The efficacy of medication in alleviating symptoms of mental illnesses and the compatibility of medication with non-pharmacological therapy serve as key components in constructing a comprehensive and effective treatment plan for patients. Medication is not the last resort but a crucial instrument in managing mental health issues.

9

Based on the texts, how would the author of Text 1 most likely respond to the underlined statement in Text 2?

(A) By making claims regarding the advantages of implementing lifestyle changes in contrast to engaging in psychological therapies

(B) By acknowledging the pressing need for swift and effective interventions when addressing severe mental health conditions

(C) By emphasizing the importance of pursuing alternative treatments for mental health disorders, considering the potential drawbacks associated with medication

(D) By conceding that the positive outcomes gained from easing symptoms with medication might surpass the potential risks associated with adverse side effects

SCORE SHAKE

Back   Next

Esteemed as a treasure among citrus fruits, the lemon captivates with its vivid yellow color and enticing aroma that fills the air, offering a delightful sensory experience. Its tangy, acidic pulp, enclosed by a thick, textured rind, presents abundant culinary and medicinal applications. Beyond these qualities, the rich history of this small fruit adds an element of intrigue. Originating in the lush groves of ancient Persia, lemons have journeyed across the world, leaving a lasting impression on the culinary traditions of numerous cultures. Consequently, with its diverse uses, the lemon continues to fascinate and charm those who venture to discover its complexities.

10

According to the text, what characteristic of the lemon has contributed most to its impact on the food traditions of various cultures?

(A) Its captivating and vivid yellow color that fills the air with delight

(B) The fascinating past of this petite fruit contributing to an air of mystery

(C) The zesty, sour pulp surrounded by a robust peel, which lends itself to various culinary and therapeutic uses

(D) The sturdy, coarse outer layer that envelops the acidic pulp, adding to its distinctive visual appeal

SCORE SHAKE

Back   Next

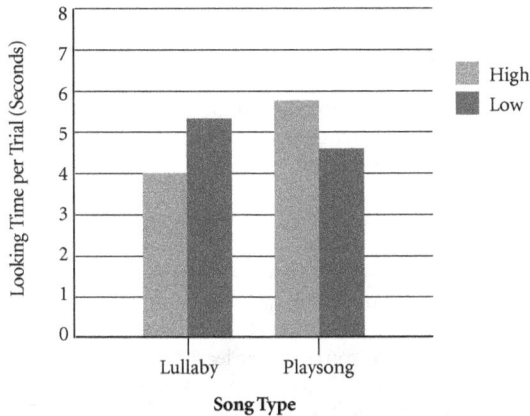

Song Type

Lullabies, the ultimate mood-setters for the little ones! But have you ever wondered what makes them so appealing to newborns? It turns out that preverbal infants are highly sensitive to the emotional nuances conveyed through lullabies and playsongs. Yet, the exact singing characteristics that give rise to this sensitivity are still a mystery. To shed some light on this, Christine Tsang and Nicole Conrad from Saint Mary's University conducted a study on 6- and 7-month-old infants, using a head-turn preference approach. The infants were presented with various lullabies and playsongs with different pitches. The researchers then observed and recorded the infants' head turns towards the source of the sounds. By analyzing the frequency and duration of these head turns, the researchers could determine the infants' preferences for specific pitches in the songs. The results showed that babies have a natural preference for low-pitched lullabies and high-pitched playsongs.

11

Which choice best describes data from the graph that support the researchers' conclusion?

(A) Babies took more time to gaze at the source of lullabies and playsongs when lower-pitched songs were played.

(B) When listening to lower-pitched lullabies, babies turned their heads five times, compared to four times for high-pitched lullabies; however, the opposite pattern occurred for playsongs.

(C) Infants spent an average of five seconds gazing at the source of low-pitched lullabies and four seconds at high-pitched ones; for playsongs, they spent just over five seconds on high-pitched songs and 4.2 seconds on low-pitched ones.

(D) The looking times for both high- and low-pitched lullabies and playsongs were similar, indicating no preference for less frequently heard lullabies.

"*The Going*" is an early 1900s poem by Thomas Hardy in which he refers to his recently departed wife. In the poem, the speaker describes the feeling of being able to briefly detect her presence: _____

12

Which quotation from the poem best illustrates the claim?

(A) "Why did you give no hint that night / That quickly after the morrow's dawn, / And calmly as if indifferent quite / You would close your term here, up and be gone?"

(B) "Never to bid good-bye / Or lip me the softest call, / Or utter a wish for a word, while I / Saw morning harden upon the wall"

(C) "Why do you make me leave the house / And think for a breath it is you I see / At the end of the alley of bending boughs / Where so often at dusk you used to be"

(D) "Well, well! All's past amend, / Unchangeable. It must go. / I seem but a dead man held on end"

Back　Next

The Uncertainty Principle, proposed by Werner Heisenberg, states that we cannot measure the position and momentum of a subatomic particle with absolute certainty. This principle led to the development of quantum mechanics, which has revolutionized our understanding of the behavior of particles at the subatomic level. One significant application of the principles of quantum mechanics is in the design and operation of MRI (Magnetic Resonance Imaging) machines used in medical imaging. MRI machines use powerful magnetic fields to manipulate the behavior of electrons in the body, and the principles of quantum mechanics help to explain how these electrons behave in response to the magnetic fields.

13

According to the text, what is the relationship between the Uncertainty Principle and the development of MRI technology?

(A) The Uncertainty Principle is not related to the development of MRI technology, as MRI machines operate on other principles.

(B) The Uncertainty Principle led to the development of quantum mechanics, which in turn led to the design and operation of MRI machines.

(C) Heisenberg was inspired to conceive the Uncertainty Principle based on his discovery of the principles of quantum mechanics, which were instrumental in developing MRI technology.

(D) The MRI machine is a medical device that was greatly improved due to Heisenberg's Uncertainty Principle.

Back　Next

The songs of a nightingale, the laughter of children playing, and the melody of a jazz band are all examples of beautiful sounds that evoke a sense of joy and harmony. Each of these distinct sounds, whether from nature or human-made sources, contributes to the richness of the auditory tapestry that surrounds us. The diversity and beauty of these sounds are essential to our appreciation of the world and our emotional well-being. Hence, _____

14

Which choice most logically completes the text?

(A) learning to play an instrument can serve as a powerful reminder of the joy and harmony that music brings, enriching individuals' lives and fostering emotional well-being.

(B) the soothing sounds of nature often provide greater satisfaction to listeners compared to man-made noises.

(C) the ability to differentiate between various sounds is crucial for effective communication and comprehension in our daily lives.

(D) it is important to preserve and celebrate the vast array of auditory experiences available to us.

III

France's mandatory school attendance until the age 16 or 18 exemplifies an education policy that acknowledges the crucial role of compulsory education in promoting national economic and social progress. By immersing students in diverse perspectives and experiences through required schooling, the students develop a heightened sense of social cohesion and tolerance. Furthermore, it is a well-established fact that a well-educated population is vital for a nation's prosperity. An elevated level of public education results in a more proficient workforce, which subsequently fuels economic growth. As _____, the implementation and preservation of such policies in countries like France ensure the cultivation of a flourishing society.

15

Which choice most logically completes the text?

(A) mandatory education enhances and elevates the overall education of a nation

(B) students gain valuable emotional support through the encouragement and guidance offered by their classmates and mentors

(C) students acknowledge that the knowledge they gain from school is comparable to what they learn at home

(D) educators, who devote their time and expertise to instructing students, comprise a notable and substantial segment of the labor force

Section 1, Module 2: Reading and Writing

Directions ∨

Annotate   More

The World Baseball Classic, an international tournament, brings together elite players, national pride, and thrilling competition. This quadrennial event, established in 2006, unites countries such as the United States, a powerhouse in _____ a dominant force; and the Dominican Republic, known for its passion for baseball. The contest, a display of skill and determination, captivates fans worldwide.

16

Which choice completes the text so that it conforms to the conventions of Standard English?

(A) the sport; Japan,

(B) the sport, Japan,

(C) the sport, Japan;

(D) the sport; Japan

Back   Next

Section 1, Module 2: Reading and Writing

Directions ∨

Annotate   More

Desert plants exhibit remarkable anatomical adaptations to thrive in arid environments. Possessing thick, fleshy leaves or stems, they store water for extended periods of drought. By opening their stomata at night, _____ Additionally, extensive root systems enable them to efficiently absorb scarce water resources, ensuring survival in harsh conditions.

17

Which choice completes the text so that it conforms to the conventions of Standard English?

(A) the amount of water lost by these plants can be minimized through transpiration.

(B) minimum water loss is possible through transpiration for these plants.

(C) transpiration is how these plants ensure minimum water loss.

(D) these plants minimize water loss through transpiration.

Back   Next

Insurance companies and commercial banks maintain a symbiotic relationship, often collaborating to offer a wide range of financial services. Banks may distribute insurance products, generating additional revenue streams for both parties. Insurance companies, in turn, invest their premiums in various assets, including bank deposits, ensuring a stable source of funds for banks and fostering mutual _____ benefiting from the partnership.

18

Which choice completes the text so that it conforms to the conventions of Standard English?

- (A) growth, both industries
- (B) growth, and both industries
- (C) growth. Both industries
- (D) growth; both industries

SCORE SHAKE

Back Next

White blood cells (WBCs), _____ defend our bodies against harmful pathogens. A person's WBC count reflects their immune system's strength. Elevated WBC levels may indicate infection or inflammation, while low levels can suggest a weakened immune response. Infections' symptoms and severity vary, highlighting the importance of maintaining a healthy balance of WBCs for an individual's well-being.

19

Which choice completes the text so that it conforms to the conventions of Standard English?

- (A) the human immune systems crucial components,
- (B) the human immune systems crucial component's,
- (C) the human immune system's crucial components,
- (D) the human immune system's crucial components',

SCORE SHAKE

Back Next

In 1992, a shipping container filled with thousands of rubber ducks and other plastic bath toys was accidentally released into the Pacific Ocean. These rubber ducks, often referred to as "friendly floaties," began washing up on shores across the globe. Even more spectacular than that of traditional tracking methods, _____ and their influence on the distribution of debris. The rubber ducky phenomenon has since captured the public's imagination and shed light on the interconnectedness of our oceans.

20

Which choice completes the text so that it conforms to the conventions of Standard English?

- (A) the rubber ducks were a crucial part of attaining valuable insights into ocean currents
- (B) these friendly floaties provided valuable insights into ocean currents
- (C) this unintentional experiment provided valuable insights into ocean currents
- (D) the valuable insights gained from this unusual phenomenon were introduced to oceanographers

Post-traumatic stress disorder (PTSD) is a mental health condition triggered by experiencing or witnessing a traumatic event. Individuals with PTSD often suffer from anxiety, flashbacks, and nightmares. Therapies such as cognitive-behavioral therapy and exposure therapy may be employed _____ and treat PTSD, helping sufferers regain a sense of control over their lives.

21

Which choice completes the text so that it conforms to the conventions of Standard English?

- (A) managing
- (B) to manage
- (C) are managing
- (D) managed

The darkroom plays a crucial role in traditional film photography development. It provides a light-controlled environment, allowing photographers to process film without damaging it. With the advent of digital photography, the use of _____ photographers have shifted towards digital methods for greater convenience and efficiency.

22

Which choice completes the text so that it conforms to the conventions of Standard English?

(A) darkrooms has declined; however,

(B) darkrooms has declined however

(C) darkrooms has declined, however,

(D) darkrooms has declined, however;

In the fascinating world of plant biology, researchers often explore the role of plant hormones in regulating stem elongation in *Arabidopsis thaliana,* focusing on their direct influence on cellular growth. _____ these hormones can also be seen as the architects of plant growth, coordinating environmental responses and adaptation rather than just driving elongation. This intriguing investigation highlights plant hormones' multifaceted nature and diverse roles in governing plant development.

23

Which choice completes the text with the most logical transition?

(A) In sum,

(B) On the other hand,

(C) Instead,

(D) Regardless,

Monetary policy plays a crucial role in maintaining inflation and output stability, as central banks adjust interest rates to balance economic growth and price stability. _____ external factors such as global economic trends and geopolitical events can challenge these efforts, highlighting the importance of adaptability and vigilance in crafting effective monetary policy responses.

24

Which choice completes the text with the most logical transition?

(A) Subsequently,

(B) Specifically,

(C) Likewise,

(D) Regardless,

Section 1, Module 2: Reading and Writing

Directions ∨

32:00

Hide

Annotate   More

While researching a topic, a student has taken the following notes:

- Carnivorous plants get some of their nutrients from animals such as insects or single-celled protozoans.
- They trap their prey either through active mechanisms such as leaves that roll up around their prey or through passive mechanisms such as sticky mucilage.
- These plants typically live in areas where the soil is thin or lacks many nutrients, leading to a need for alternative sources of nutrients.
- Charles Darwin was the first person to significantly study these plants.
- At least 583 species of plants trap and kill their prey.
- About one-fourth of these plants are threatened with extinction because of human activity.

25

The student wants to emphasize the reason behind the evolution of these particular plants into carnivores. Which choice most effectively uses relevant information from the notes to accomplish this goal?

(A) Darwin was the first person to significantly study carnivorous plants.

(B) Of the 583 species of plants that trap and kill their prey, about one-fourth of these plants are threatened with extinction because of human activity.

(C) Since some plants live in areas where the soil is thin or lacks many nutrients, the plants get some of their nutrients from animals such as insects or single-celled protozoans.

(D) Carnivorous plants get some of their nutrients either through active mechanisms such as leaves that roll up around their prey or through passive mechanisms such as sticky mucilage.

While researching a topic, a student has taken the following notes:

- Ursula K. Le Guin is the author of *The Left Hand of Darkness*, a science fiction novel published in 1969.
- The story is set in a fictional universe known as Hanish.
- The book was one of the first in the genre known as feminist science fiction.
- It was a commercial and critical success and was considered by many to be a work of high literature, not just of science fiction.
- Le Guin's interest in ecology and her concerns regarding nuclear weapons are evident in the book.

26

The student wants to introduce *The Left Hand of Darkness* to an audience unfamiliar with the work and its author. Which choice most effectively uses relevant information from the notes to accomplish this goal?

(A) Ursula K. Le Guin, the author of *The Left Hand of Darkness*, experienced both commercial and critical acclaim following the book's publication.

(B) Written by Ursula K. Le Guin, *The Left Hand of Darkness* is a work of science fiction that reflects the author's interest in ecology and her concerns regarding nuclear weapons.

(C) When the book was published in 1969, the genre of feminist science fiction had few predecessors to *The Left Hand of Darkness*.

(D) Many people regard *The Left Hand of Darkness* to be a work of high literature and not just of science fiction.

While researching a topic, a student has taken the following notes:

- A clinical trial with over 20,000 adults in the United States was conducted by a medical school.
- Participants were given cocoa extract supplements, multivitamins, or a placebo daily for about 3.5 years.
- The health of the participants was tracked during the trial.
- As a group, those who took the cocoa experienced a significant decrease in adverse cardiovascular events relative to the placebo group.
- The published study called for more research into the reasons for the reduction.

27

The student wants to present the aim of the clinical trial. Which choice most effectively uses relevant information from the notes to accomplish this goal?

(A) Participants in a clinical trial with over 20,000 adults in the United States were given daily cocoa extract supplements, multivitamins, or a placebo for about 3.5 years.

(B) The effects of taking cocoa extract supplements, multivitamins, or a placebo daily on cardiovascular and overall health were investigated.

(C) There was a significant decrease in adverse cardiovascular health events in participants given cocoa extract supplements.

(D) The published study on a clinical trial given to over 20,000 adults in the United States conducted by a medical school called for more research into the reasons for a reduction in adverse cardiovascular events in participants who took a cocoa extract supplement.

| \multicolumn{3}{c}{TEST 3 Module 1} |||
No.	Answer	Question Type
1	D	Text Completion
2	B	Text Completion
3	B	Text Completion
4	C	Text Completion
5	A	Vocabulary in Context
6	D	Main Purpose / Poem
7	C	Main Idea
8	C	Main Purpose
9	A	Cross-Text
10	D	Direct Comprehension
11	B	Command of Evidence / Quantitative
12	C	Command of Evidence / Quantitative
13	A	Command of Evidence / Textual
14	B	Inference
15	B	Conventions of Standard English
16	B	Conventions of Standard English
17	A	Conventions of Standard English
18	C	Conventions of Standard English
19	D	Conventions of Standard English
20	B	Conventions of Standard English
21	A	Conventions of Standard English
22	A	Transition
23	B	Transition
24	A	Note Summary
25	D	Note Summary
26	C	Note Summary
27	B	Note Summary

| \multicolumn{3}{c}{TEST 3 Module 2} |||
No.	Answer	Question Type
1	D	Text Completion
2	A	Text Completion
3	B	Text Completion
4	A	Text Completion
5	B	Vocabulary in Context
6	C	Main Purpose / Poem
7	B	Function / Literature
8	C	Structure / Poem
9	C	Cross-text
10	C	Direct Comprehension
11	C	Command of Evidence / Quantitative
12	C	Command of Evidence / Literature
13	B	Direct Comprehension
14	D	Inference
15	A	Inference
16	A	Conventions of Standard English
17	D	Conventions of Standard English
18	A	Conventions of Standard English
19	C	Conventions of Standard English
20	C	Conventions of Standard English
21	B	Conventions of Standard English
22	D	Conventions of Standard English
23	B	Transition
24	D	Transition
25	C	Note Summary
26	B	Note Summary
27	B	Note Summary

DIGITAL SAT Advanced SCORING CHART
Raw score to Score Conversion Chart

Raw Score	Score		Incorrect	Score
54	800		26	530
53	770		25	530
52	740		24	510
51	730		23	510
50	710		22	490
49	710		21	480
48	690		20	480
47	680		19	460
46	680		18	450
45	670		17	430
44	660		16	400
43	650		15	380
42	630		14	360
41	630		13	340
40	620		12	330
39	620		11	310
38	620		10	300
37	610		9	280
36	600		8	260
35	600		7	260
34	590		6	250
33	590		5	240
32	580		4	220
31	580		3	200
30	570		2	200
29	560		1	200
28	550		0	200
27	540			

Digital SAT
Practice Test #IV

IV

Section 1, Module 1: Reading and Writing

32:00

Directions

Hide

Annotate   More

The questions in this section address a number of important reading and writing skills. Each question includes one or more passages, which may include a table or graph. Read each passage and question carefully, and then choose the best answer to the question based on the text(s).

All questions in this section are multiple-choice with four answer choices. Each question has a single best answer.

Section 1, Module 1: Reading and Writing

Directions ∨

Annotate   More

Studies have shown that exposure to idealized images of beauty and body types can lead to negative perceptions of one's own body. One of the studies shows that young women who spend more time on social media are more likely to experience body _____. This finding underscores the need for interventions to help young people develop skills to cope with the negative impact of social media.

1

Which choice completes the text with the most logical and precise word or phrase?

(A) contentment

(B) appreciation

(C) transformation

(D) dissatisfaction

SCORE SHAKE

Next

Section 1, Module 1: Reading and Writing

Directions ∨

Annotate   More

While the idea of feathered dinosaurs may seem unusual, the discovery of the species *Ubirajara jubatus* in Brazil adds to the _____ body of evidence supporting their existence. The unique fur-like structures of *Ubirajara* provide important insights into the diversity and complexity of feathered dinosaurs and the evolution of feathers themselves.

2

Which choice completes the text with the most logical and precise word or phrase?

(A) mounting

(B) foreign

(C) nonexistent

(D) obvious

SCORE SHAKE

Back   Next

Studying the influence of Renaissance painting on modern art is important for understanding the evolution of art over the centuries. Examining the techniques, style, and subject matter of Renaissance painting allows us to gain _____ how these elements have impacted the development of modern art.

3

Which choice completes the text with the most logical and precise word or phrase?

- (A) technique for
- (B) insight into
- (C) approval of
- (D) questions for

Back　Next

Classic and contemporary children's literature continues to reinforce gender stereotypes, perpetuating the portrayal of male characters as active and assertive, female characters as passive and nurturing. Such stereotypical _____ can impact children's attitudes and beliefs about gender roles and restrict their aspirations and opportunities.

4

Which choice completes the text with the most logical and precise word or phrase?

- (A) acknowledgments
- (B) efforts
- (C) contention
- (D) representations

Back　Next

Section 1, Module 1: Reading and Writing
Directions ∨

32:00
Hide

Annotate   More

This text has been adapted from a 1979 novel, *The Ghost Writer*, written by the American author Philip Roth.

She sensed that the calm routine of her daily life was in keeping with the tranquility that had characterized life on the farm for six generations. The present and past felt less like separate entities and more like interchangeable concepts. She didn't need a time machine to understand her grandparents' lives. Instead, she found parallels between her own experiences and those of her grandfather, recognizing similarities between their lives in the same unchanging setting.
…
The town of Milton was dim and gentle, molded by gentle lives, the current of change as slow through it as the seep of water through a bog.

5

Which choice best describes the function of the underlined sentence in the text as a whole?

(A) It conveys a sense of the deliberate pace of life in Milton.

(B) It evokes the natural setting of the town of Milton.

(C) It imparts a perception of confinement that the author felt in Milton.

(D) It creates an impression of vague foreboding.

SCORE SHAKE

Question 5 of 27 ∧

Back   Next

Section 1, Module 1: Reading and Writing
Directions ∨

32:00
Hide

Annotate   More

The following text is from Ella Wheeler Wilcox's 1896 poem "*High Noon*." The phrase "warp and woof" refers to the way in which fabrics are woven.

Have I done nobly? Then I must not let
Dead yesterday unborn to-morrow shame.
Have I done wrong? Well, let the bitter taste
Of fruit that turned to ashes on my lip
Be my reminder in temptation's hour,
And keep me silent when I would condemn.
Nothing that is not there and the nothing that is.

6

According to the passage, behaving badly leads the speaker to which of the following?

(A) Regretting the past

(B) Working hard in the present

(C) Taking action with vigor

(D) Not being critical of others

SCORE SHAKE

Question 6 of 27 ∧

Back   Next

Section 1, Module 1: Reading and Writing
Directions ∨

32:00
Hide

Annotate More

The discovery of the species of ancient turtle *Arvinachelys goldeni* shed new light on the evolution of turtles during the Late Triassic period. The well-preserved fossils of the species provided new insights into the morphology and anatomy of early turtles, helping to fill gaps in our understanding of turtle evolution during this time. Specifically, the discovery suggested that early turtles had more diverse body plans and shell structures than previously thought, and that the evolution of turtle diversity may have been more complex than previously assumed.

7

Which choice best states the main purpose of the text?

(A) To explain how the discovery of the species of ancient turtle has contributed to a more comprehensive understanding of the evolution of turtles

(B) To provide a detailed analysis of the recent discovery of a species of ancient turtle and its significance in our understanding of the history of life on Earth

(C) To demonstrate the importance of paleontological discoveries, such as the recent discovery of a species of ancient turtle, in furthering our understanding of the natural world

(D) To explore the unique features and morphology of *Arvinachelys goldeni* and the complex nature of its diversification

The following text is from British poet Fay Inchfawn's poem "*In Convalescence.*" Someone who is in convalescence is getting better from being sick.

Not long ago, I prayed for dying grace,
For then I thought to see Thee face to face.

And now I ask (Lord, 'tis a weakling's cry)
That Thou wilt give me grace to live, not die.

Such foolish prayers! I know. Yet pray I must.
Lord help me help me not to see the dust!

And not to nag, nor fret because the blind
Hangs crooked, and the curtain sags behind.

But, oh! The kitchen cupboards! What a sight!
'T'will take at least a month to get them right.

And that last cocoa had a smoky taste,
And all the milk has boiled away to waste!

And no, I resolutely will not think
About the saucepans, nor about the sink.

These light afflictions are but temporal things
To rise above them, wilt Thou lend me wings?

8

Which is the main idea of the text?

(A) The speaker wishes that she had not prayed for dying grace now that she is getting well.

(B) The speaker believes that her health will improve if she doesn't think about all the household chores that need to be addressed.

(C) The speaker feels guilty that she has spent so much time bothered by small matters and not enough on spiritual matters.

(D) The speaker, now that she is no longer very sick, prays to not be overly bothered by relatively trivial household problems.

Text 1

The stock market has only existed for about a century, but it's a powerful wealth-creating tool and the epitome of capitalism. It allows people of any social class to invest in influential companies and have a say in future business decisions. This gives it the potential to impact economies worldwide.

Text 2

For almost a century, the stock market has been accused, rightly, of attracting unscrupulous individuals who take advantage of unsuspecting investors. The promise that individual shareholders can have a say in the direction of large corporations is more theoretical than actual. In reality, individual investors often suffer financial losses, while wealthy stock market analysts and professional traders benefit. Historical events such as the Great Depression highlight the risks associated with investing in the stock market.

9

Based on the texts, what would the author of Text 2 most likely say about Text 1's characterization of the stock market?

(A) The Great Depression illustrates the enduring fortitude of individuals when confronted with prolonged challenges.

(B) In recent times, individual investors have gained more influence, and they have the potential to impact the global economy.

(C) The statement is flawed as the stock market is controlled by affluent individuals and analysts deceive investors.

(D) The stock market embodies the fundamental principles of capitalism, offering a level playing field for all participants.

A

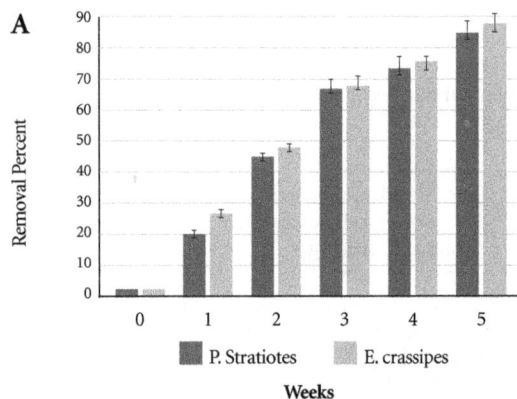

B

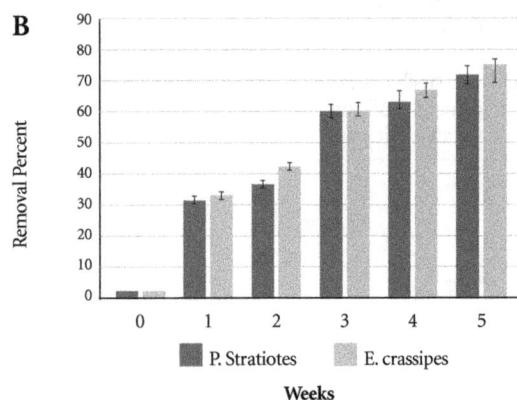

Phytoremediation is a technology that employs plants and their associated microbes to remove pollutants from contaminated soils and waters. Utilizing this technique is an acceptable, low-cost, simple, and common wastewater treatment method. Yudha Gusti Wibowo et al. analyzed the potential of phytoremediation to treat a combination of various types of wastewater in the laboratory under environmental control. The plants *Pistia stratiotes* and *Eichhornia crassipes* were used in this phytoremediation research with the goal of removing heavy metals from the wastewater, such as Fe (A) and Mn (B). The researchers claim that both *Eichhornia crassipes* and *Pistia stratiotes* showed high removal efficiency.

10

Which choice best describes data in the graph that support the researcher's conclusion?

(A) *Pistia stratiotes and Eichhornia crassipes* successfully reduced heavy metals Fe up to 89% and Mn up to 74% in a span of 5 weeks.

(B) E. crassipes was slightly less efficient in the phytoremediation of Fe and Mn than P. stratiotes.

(C) The amount of phytoremediation produced by Pistia stratiotes and Eichhornia crassipes for both metals is the highest at week 3.

(D) Phytoremediation is not a practical technique because both microbes are not successful in the removal of heavy metals at week 0.

Section 1, Module 1: Reading and Writing

Directions ⌄

32:00
Hide

✎ Annotate

⋮ More

A Man Called Ove by Fredrik Backman is a novel written in 1981. In the novel, the author implies that the narrator was raised in a rural environment: _____.

11

Which quotation from *A Man Called Ove* most effectively illustrates the claim?

(A) "My aunt and my Uncle Victor lived in Peterborough, halfway to Winnipeg. Peterborough had a town square with several steeples and a number of huge brick buildings that stood like giants, bigger than silos."

(B) "We parked and walked past the storefronts, my mother and I. Though I knew the answer, I asked for a leather baseball glove in the window of the toy shop."

(C) "She eyed the glove in the interior of the hardware store. She leaned close enough to the window to tip her hat. It was her only hat, made of light straw, with two large purple plastic orchids. She typically wore it at Easter."

(D) "She was pretty and looked much younger than Mother. She indeed wore white gloves, as Mother predicted. She stroked my cheek, and she offered me chocolates from a glass bowl."

The National Institutes of Health conducted a study on the effects of a plant-based diet on cardiovascular disease risk factors. The study followed participants over a year and found that those on the plant-based diet had significantly lower blood pressure and cholesterol levels than those on the control diet. They also had lower body weights and body fat percentages. These results suggest that a plant-based diet can lead to significant reductions in cardiovascular disease risk factors and should be recommended as part of a healthy diet. Further research, however, is needed to understand the mechanisms behind this effect.

12

Which finding, if true, would most strongly support the Institute's prediction?

(A) Those on the plant-based diet consumed more healthy fats than did the control group.

(B) The study showed an average 10-point reduction in blood pressure levels for participants on the plant-based diet.

(C) The participants who were on the plant-based increased their physical activity, leading to a decrease in cholesterol levels.

(D) Consuming fewer processed and refined foods lowered cholesterol levels in all the participants of the study.

13

Which choice most logically completes the text?

(A) there is no point in pursuing these goals, because they would ultimately prove impossible to carry out.

(B) absolute equity is not possible, yet I still believe that some improvement is possible.

(C) I do not care about what is realistically possible but am only concerned with the way that things should be.

(D) even though property cannot be divided equally, it should still be divided according to a man's abilities.

Some astronomers believe that dark matter is the elusive substance that makes up the majority of the universe's missing mass. Previously, astronomers believed that interstellar space was largely empty and transparent. However, the development of photography revealed a complex structure of star clouds, rifts, and holes where few or no stars existed. As research progressed, it became apparent that these features were clouds of obscuring material, now referred to as dark matter. Initially, astronomers were hesitant to accept the presence of dark matter. This was because the absorbing dust could dim the light of distant stars and make it difficult for researchers to determine the locations and brightness of stars. This obstacle proved to be a significant challenge for astronomers and in fact _____.

14

Which choice most logically completes the text?

- (A) dark matter would have detrimental effects on the Milky Way
- (B) photography would actually complicate the work of scientists
- (C) dark matter would change some fundamental beliefs about astronomy
- (D) dark matter would make it easier to determine a star's distance

French Impressionism art was the first modern artistic style to produce significant masterpieces inspired by real life. French Impressionist artists rejected classical subject matter in favor of _____ to create works that represented their current circumstances and environments.

15

Which choice completes the text so that it conforms to the conventions of Standard English?

- (A) modernity seeking
- (B) modernity, seeking
- (C) modernity; seeking
- (D) modernity. Seeking

Section 1, Module 1: Reading and Writing

Directions ⌄

Annotate   More

Ascending the steep mountain, _____ The rugged terrain and rocky outcroppings gave way to a sweeping view of rolling hills and dense forests. The hiker felt a sense of awe and reverence for the natural world.

16

Which choice completes the text so that it conforms to the conventions of Standard English?

- (A) the intrepid hiker marveled at the panoramic vista stretching before her.
- (B) the panoramic vista stretching before the intrepid hiker surprised her.
- (C) there was an intrepid hiker who marveled at the panoramic vista stretching before her.
- (D) the marvels of the panoramic vista surprised the intrepid hiker.

Section 1, Module 1: Reading and Writing

Directions ⌄

Annotate   More

The subfield of neuropsychology focuses on the relationship between the brain and behavior. Neuropsychologists study how brain damage, disease, or dysfunction can affect cognitive and emotional processes. By using neuroimaging techniques and neuropsychological assessments, _____ can pinpoint specific areas of the brain that are associated with particular functions such as memory, attention, and language.

17

Which choice completes the text so that it conforms to the conventions of Standard English?

- (A) it
- (B) we
- (C) they
- (D) he

Any New York City construction project using municipal funds _____ required to consider whether historical artifacts will be affected during construction, and if that possibility exists, an urban archaeologist must be consulted

18

Which choice completes the text so that it conforms to the conventions of Standard English?

- (A) are
- (B) have been
- (C) is
- (D) were

These days, many _____ in philosophy have no intention of becoming philosophers; instead, they plan to apply those skills to other disciplines. Law and business specifically benefit from the complicated theoretical issues raised in the study of philosophy.

19

Which choice completes the text so that it conforms to the conventions of Standard English?

- (A) student's majoring
- (B) students majoring
- (C) students' majoring
- (D) students major

_____ uncovered the peculiar mating rituals of the Obscurum saltans, a recently discovered nocturnal dancing beetle. This enigmatic insect, native to the dense Amazonian rainforest, engages in synchronized mid-air courtship ballets, emitting bioluminescent bursts, resulting in a mesmerizing nocturnal spectacle.

20

Which choice completes the text so that it conforms to the conventions of Standard English?

(A) Researchers Dr. Lila Hopper, and Dr. Hugo Stanton

(B) Researchers, Dr. Lila Hopper and Dr. Hugo Stanton,

(C) Researchers, Dr. Lila Hopper and Dr. Hugo Stanton;

(D) Researchers Dr. Lila Hopper and Dr. Hugo Stanton

Back   Next

Scientists harnessed the power of a synchrotron to probe atomic behavior, revealing unparalleled insights into matter. By accelerating charged particles at near-light speeds, the synchrotron generates brilliant X-rays, enabling researchers to visualize atoms dancing, bonding, and reacting, thereby _____ the secrets of materials at the most fundamental level.

21

Which choice completes the text so that it conforms to the conventions of Standard English?

(A) unlocks

(B) unlocking

(C) to unlock

(D) was unlocking

Back   Next

Section 1, Module 1: Reading and Writing

Directions ⌄

32:00
Hide

Annotate   More

George Washington was a visionary leader who played a pivotal role in shaping the nation's history. His military prowess and political acumen were instrumental in the American _____ his unwavering commitment to democracy and civic duty set the standard for future presidents.

22

Which choice completes the text so that it conforms to the conventions of Standard English?

(A) Revolution,

(B) Revolution and

(C) Revolution, and

(D) Revolution; and

Section 1, Module 1: Reading and Writing

Directions ⌄

32:00
Hide

Annotate   More

Art history studies visual arts, including painting, sculpture, architecture, and other forms of artistic expression. It seeks to understand the stylistic and cultural influences that shape the creation and reception of art throughout history. _____ art history involves the analysis of individual works of art and broader historical and cultural contexts that shape artistic movements and trends.

23

Which choice completes the text with the most logical transition?

(A) As a result,

(B) Instead,

(C) To conclude,

(D) Furthermore,

IV

Percy Julian, a renowned chemist and pioneer for African Americans in science, made significant contributions to synthetic, organic, and medicinal chemistry. Julian's groundbreaking research on plant alkaloids led to the synthesis of numerous life-saving drugs, including cortisone and progesterone. _____ he faced significant barriers and discrimination throughout his career, including being denied tenure and experiencing racism in his personal life.

24

Which choice completes the text with the most logical transition?

(A) Instead,

(B) Nevertheless,

(C) Secondly,

(D) In fact,

The Navajo Nation in the southwestern United States is the largest Native American reservation, covering over 27,000 square miles. The Navajo people have a rich cultural heritage reflected in their language, arts, and traditions. _____ the Nation faces significant economic and social challenges, including high poverty rates and limited access to healthcare and education.

25

Which choice completes the text with the most logical transition?

(A) In other words,

(B) For instance,

(C) By contrast,

(D) Accordingly,

Section 1, Module 1: Reading and Writing

Directions ⌄

32:00
Hide

Annotate   More

Stomata, tiny pores on plant leaves, are essential for gas exchange, water regulation, and photosynthesis. _____ they profoundly impact plant productivity and survival. Understanding the mechanisms that control stomata behavior is critical for developing strategies to improve plant resilience to changing climates and water availability.

26

Which choice completes the text with the most logical transition?

- (A) For instance,
- (B) However,
- (C) Similarly,
- (D) As a result,

While researching a topic, a student has taken the following notes:

- Studying stimulus and response is a central theme in psychology and neuroscience.
- Researchers use a variety of experimental methods to explore relationships between sensory input and behavioral or neural output.
- These methods include behavioral assays, electrophysiological recordings, and brain imaging techniques.
- Manipulating different aspects of a stimulus helps uncover the underlying mechanisms that govern the processing and integration of sensory information.
- Understanding the complex relationship between stimuli and responses has implications for cognitive psychology, psychophysics, and clinical psychology.

27

The student wants to emphasize the significance of understanding the relationship between stimuli and responses. Which choice most effectively uses relevant information from the notes to accomplish this goal?

- (A) Researchers use various methods to explore relationships between stimuli and responses.
- (B) By manipulating various stimulus features, researchers can reveal the fundamental mechanisms that control the handling and merging of sensory information.
- (C) Neuroscience is one of the fields that require studying the stimulus and response.
- (D) Comprehending the intricate connection between stimuli and responses is crucial for clinical psychology, cognitive psychology, and psychophysics.

SCORE
SHAKE

scoreshake.com

Practice Test Break

You can resume this practice test as soon as you're ready to move on. On test day, you'll wait until the clock counts down.

Take a Break

You may leave the room, but do not disturb students who are still testing.

Do not exit the app or close your device.

Testing won't resume until you return.

Follow these rules during the break:

1. Do not access your phone, smartwatch, textbooks, notes, or the internet.

2. Do not eat or drink in the test room.

3. Do not speak in the test room; outside the test room, do not discuss the exam with anyone.

Remaing Break Time:

9:52

Resume Testing

Contemporary artists often use texture to create unique and instinctive experiences for their audience. The use of texture in artwork gives the audience a more _____ and tactile experience of the artwork, creating a more meaningful connection with the piece.

1

Which choice completes the text with the most logical and precise word or phrase?

- (A) visceral
- (B) pragmatic
- (C) abstract
- (D) sobering

The gut microbiome of honeybees plays a crucial role in their immune system, digestion, and metabolism; it is essential for maintaining the health and survival of bee colonies. Changes in the gut microbiome composition and diversity can lead to dysbiosis and _____ the immune function of bees, making them more vulnerable to diseases and environmental stressors.

2

Which choice completes the text with the most logical and precise word or phrase?

- (A) augment
- (B) denigrate
- (C) underscore
- (D) compromise

Section 1, Module 2: Reading and Writing

Directions ⌄

32:00
Hide

Annotate   More

The indigenous Maori populace of New Zealand was subjected to British colonial rule in the 19th century, giving rise to substantial cultural, social, and economic _____ of Maori communities and their intangible cultural heritage. The British superimposed novel legal, theological, and sociocultural frameworks on Maori culture, engendering the dispossession of Maori land, language, and customs.

3

Which choice completes the text with the most logical and precise word or phrase?

(A) revamps

(B) obliteration

(C) sophistications

(D) transformations

SCORE SHAKE

Question 3 of 27 ⌃

Back   Next

Section 1, Module 2: Reading and Writing

Directions ⌄

32:00
Hide

Annotate   More

The cinematic work "The Great Gatsby" directed by Baz Luhrmann employs _____ framework wherein vivid hues such as gold and yellow evoke a sense of optimism, lavishness, and profligacy, while cooler shades of blue and green connote sadness, melancholy, and disenchantment. Furthermore, Luhrmann employs lighting techniques, such as low-key lighting to proffer shadows and high contrast in order to create a feeling of inscrutability, tension, and jeopardy.

4

Which choice completes the text with the most logical and precise word or phrase?

(A) an enlightened

(B) a chromatic

(C) a temporal

(D) a digressive

SCORE SHAKE

Question 4 of 27 ⌃

Back   Next

Mosquitoes are the main "vector species" responsible for <u>propagating</u> numerous deadly diseases, including malaria, dengue, and chikungunya. Eradicating disease-carrying mosquito species would mean saving millions of human lives, as well as billions of dollars.

5

As used in the text, what does the word "propagating" most nearly mean?

(A) disseminating

(B) evolving

(C) creating

(D) prolonging

The following text is from Sir John Collings Squire's 1917 poem "*Airship Over Suburb*," published in 1922. An airship is a large, rounded aircraft sometimes called a blimp or zeppelin. Certain words use British spellings.

A smooth blue sky with puffed motionless clouds.

Standing over the plain of red roofs and bushy trees
The bright coloured shell of the large enamelled sky.

Out of the distance pointing, a cut dark shape
That moves this way at leisure, then hesitates and turns:
And its darkness suddenly dies as it turns and shows
A gleaming silver, white against even the whitest cloud.

Across the blue and the low small clouds it moves
Level, with a floating cloud-like motion of its own,
Peaceful, sunny and slow, a thing of summer itself,
Above the basking earth, travelling the clouds and the sky.

6

Which choice best states the main purpose of the text?

(A) To impress the reader with the size and shape of the airship

(B) To describe the airship as if it were a part of the natural world

(C) To illustrate the manner in which airships navigate the skies

(D) To persuade the reader that airships are especially beautiful in the summer

Section 1, Module 2: Reading and Writing

32:00
Hide

Annotate   More

The following text is from the 20th century British poet Elizabeth Jenning's poem "*In Memory Of Anyone Unknown To Me.*" An "epitaph" is a speech or phrase used to honor the dead.

At this particular time I have no one
Particular person to grieve for, though there must
Be many, many unknown ones going to dust
Slowly, not remembered for what they have done
Or left undone. For these, then, I will grieve
Being impartial, unable to deceive.

How they lived, or died, is quite unknown,
And, by that fact gives my grief purity,
An important person quite apart from me
Or one obscure who drifted down alone.
. . .

Sentiment will creep in. I cast it out
Wishing to give these classical repose,
No epitaph, no poppy and no rose
From me, and certainly no wish to learn about
The way they lived or died. In earth or fire
They are gone. Simply because they were human, I admire.

7

Which choice best describes the overall structure of the text?

- (A) The speaker explains her thinking about a course of action, gives the reason for this, and then dares others to convince her to do otherwise.

- (B) The speaker describes her current behavior, anticipates objections to this behavior, and then sums up her reasons for the behavior.

- (C) The speaker states what she will do, elaborates on this, and finally makes explicit the reason for what she plans to do.

- (D) The speaker reviews her recent past, connects this to her present, and makes plans for her future actions.

8

At the core of social reform in the United States during the Progressive Era was women's grassroots activism and their aspirations for a renewed civic awareness. Despite being mostly excluded from the electoral process except in school elections, white middle-class female reformers achieved a range of successes, particularly in enhancing working conditions for women and children. However, it is worth noting that child labor laws inadvertently created conflicts between women from various social classes. Reformers considered both child labor and industrial home work as similarly cruel practices that deserved to be prohibited, but, <u>as a number of women historians have recently observed, working-class mothers did not always share this view.</u>

Which choice best describes the function of the underlined sentence in the overall structure of the passage?

(A) It provides support for an assertion made in the preceding sentence.

(B) It presents an opinion that contests a claim made in its opening line.

(C) It highlights an inconsistency embedded within the conventional understanding of child labor reform.

(D) It proposes a contrasting perspective to the one attributed in the text to working-class mothers.

9

Text 1
Attempts have been made by architectural writers to discredit the garden cities on the ground that they lack "urbanity." Because the buildings in them are generously spaced and interspersed with gardens, lawns, and trees, they rarely produce the particular effect of absolute enclosure or packed picturesqueness not undeservedly admired by visitors to many ancient cities. But the garden city is, nonetheless, truly a "city." The criticism exposes the confusion and aesthetic narrow-mindedness of the critics. If the word "urbanity" is used in the simple etymological sense of "city-ness," the users unknowingly expose their ignorance of the infinite diversity that the world's cities display.

Text 2
Perhaps we need a simple litmus-paper test of the good city. Who lives there? Where is the center? What do you do when you get there? A successful urban design involves urbanity, the quality the garden city forgot. It is found in plazas and squares, in boulevards and promenades. It can be found in Rome's railroad station. When you find it, never let it go. It is the hardest thing to create anew.

Based on the texts, how would the author of text 1 most likely respond to the characterization of garden cities presented in text 1?

(A) By pointing out that recent research has shown the inadequacy of this characterization

(B) By proving that the facts of urban life support this characterization

(C) By indicating that this characterization is dismissed by most authorities

(D) By arguing that this characterization is neither accurate nor well-defined

Modern forms of slavery, such as forced labor and human trafficking, are a major problem in the global supply chains of multinational corporations. According to research conducted by the International Labour Organization (ILO), 24.9 million people are subject to forced labor and human trafficking in the garment industry. An alarming increase of 81% since 2005 is attributed to the exploitation of workers in developing countries, where labor regulations are weak and labor costs are low. As such, these countries are often used by multinational corporations as part of their global supply chains.

10

Which choice best states the main idea of the text?

(A) Slavery in today's world is a complex and far-reaching issue in the garment industry.

(B) The garment industry is an industry in which multinational corporations frequently utilize developing nations as part of their supply networks.

(C) Modern slavery exists in the global supply chains of multinational corporations.

(D) The ILO found that in some countries, up to 80% of garment workers are in forced labour.

Back   Next

When David Hollister introduced a seat belt bill in Michigan in the early 1980s that levied a fine for not buckling up, the state representative received hate mail comparing him to Hitler. At the time, only 14 percent of Americans regularly wore seat belts, even though the federal government required lap and shoulder belts in all new cars starting in 1968. Opponents of laws that require automobile drivers and passengers to wear seat belts argue that in a free society people have the right to take risks as long as the people do not harm others as a result of taking the risks. As a result, they conclude that it should be each person's decision whether or not to wear a seat belt.

11

Which finding, if true, would most seriously weaken the conclusion drawn above?

(A) Car insurance premiums for all vehicle owners are elevated due to the necessity of covering the higher incidence of injuries or fatalities among those not using seat belts.

(B) A significant number of modern vehicles come equipped with auto-fastening seat belts for front-seat occupants.

(C) States without compulsory seatbelt regulations experience a higher rate of car-related deaths compared to those that enforce such laws.

(D) In car crashes, a larger proportion of passengers who neglect to use seat belts sustain injuries compared to those who do wear them.

Back   Next

Section 1, Module 2: Reading and Writing

Directions ∨

32:00
Hide

Annotate   More

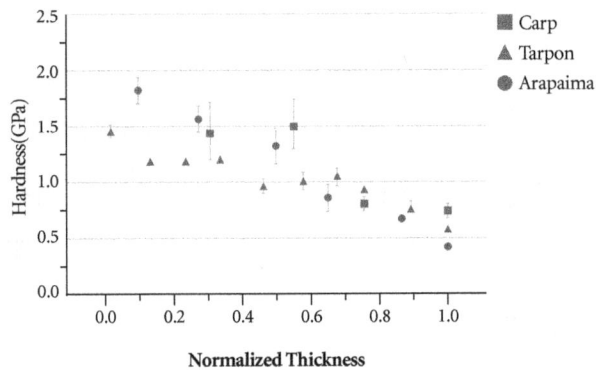

Normalized Thickness

Legend: ■ Carp ▲ Tarpon ● Arapaima

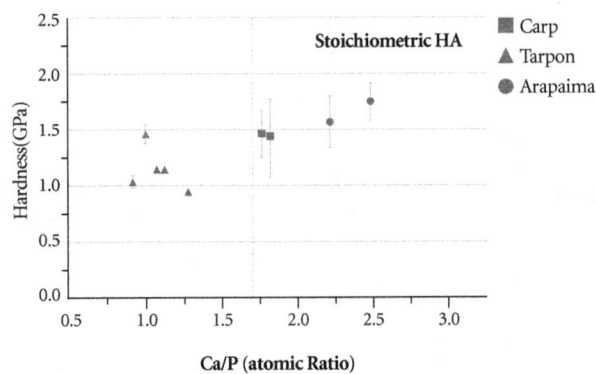

Stoichiometric HA

Ca/P (atomic Ratio)

Legend: ■ Carp ▲ Tarpon ● Arapaima

Fish scales serve as a natural armor that has impressed scientists for its flexibility. Most studies of the scales have focused on their composite structure. In contrast, little work has been done on the heavily mineralized outer layer known as the Limiting Layer (LL). This coating is crucial because it acts as the first line of defense. D. Arola's group investigated the mechanical behavior and chemical composition of the LL of 3 different fish scales – carp, tarpon, and arapaima. The calcium to phosphorus (Ca/P) ratio of the LL was found to vary among the three fish scales. Generally, the LL of tarpon scales was found to be the hardest, followed by the carp and then the arapaima, according to the results of an indentation test. The researchers claim that the differences in hardness are related to the Ca/P ratio, possibly caused by the growth rate and habitat of each species.

12

Which choice best describes data in the graph that support the researcher's conclusion?

(A) The nanoindentation results showed that the LL of tarpon scales is the hardest, correlating with the Ca/P ratio with tarpons scales as the highest, followed by the carp, and then arapaima.

(B) The nanoindentation results showed that the LL of tarpon scales is the softest, followed by the carp and the arapaima, correlating with the Ca/P ratio with tarpons scales as the lowest, followed by the carp, and then arapaima.

(C) The scales of arapaima and carp show similar hardness values, which is explained by their similar Ca/P ratio.

(D) There is no significant correlation between the hardness of the fish scale and the Ca/P ratio.

This text is adapted from a novel, "*A Respectable Woman*," by Kate Chopin written in 1894. In the novel, the author portrays Gouvernail, a close friend of Mr. Baroda, to be polite and cordial towards Mrs. Baroda but did not make any effort to impress her or get her attention: _____.

13

Which quotation from *A Respectable Woman* most effectively illustrates the claim above?

(A) "She had unconsciously formed an image of him in her mind. She pictured him tall, slim, cynical; with eye-glasses, and his hands in his pockets; and she did not like him."

(B) "She could discover in him none of those brilliant and promising traits which Gaston, her husband, had often assured her that he possessed."

(C) "His manner was as courteous toward her as the most exacting woman could require; but he made no direct appeal to her approval or even esteem."

(D) "Once settled at the plantation he seemed to like to sit upon the wide portico in the shade of one of the big Corinthian pillars, smoking his cigar lazily and listening attentively to Gaston's experience as a sugar planter."

For many years, it was thought that the advent of agriculture led early farmers to establish settlements near their fields. However, recent findings by archaeologist Arlene Rosen at Catalhoyuk, a significant Neolithic farming community in Turkey, have challenged this notion. Although Catalhoyuk was situated in marshy wetlands, Rosen's examination of fossilized wheat and barley remains suggests that the crops were grown in a dry area. Some specialists dispute the <u>idea</u> that farmers from Catalhoyuk cultivated remote fields, as this would require transporting large amounts of grain. Nonetheless, archaeobotanist Eleni Asouti has determined that the wood used in the village's construction originated more than twelve kilometers from the settlement.

14

Which of the following, if true, would most challenge the "idea?"

(A) Farmers in Catalhoyuk practiced crop rotation, changing the crops they planted each year.

(B) The farmers of Catalhoyuk utilized communal wheat and barley fields, which they shared with nearby villages.

(C) Farmers in Catalhoyuk employed wood that was susceptible to decay in the moist surroundings.

(D) The wheat and barley analyzed by Rosen were acquired by Catalhoyuk's farmers through trade.

The following text is adapted from Harriet Beecher Stowe's *The Lady Who Does Her Own Work*, issued as a chapter of Stowe's *Household Papers and Other Stories*, written in 1896.

　"The lady who does her own work."
　America is the only country where such a title is possible; the only country where there is a class of women who may be described as ladies who do their own work. By a lady we mean a woman of education, cultivation, and refinement, of liberal tastes and ideas, who, without any very material additions or changes, would be recognized as a lady in any circle of the Old World or the New.
　What I have said is that the existence of such a class is a fact peculiar to American society, a clear, plain result of the new principles involved in the doctrine of universal equality. This means that in countries other than America, _____.

15

Which choice most logically completes the text?

(A) a maid might occasionally hold equal or even surpass the authority of her mistress.

(B) in the past, feminist ideas and philosophies were largely unknown or unacknowledged.

(C) women were granted leadership roles on par with their male counterparts.

(D) the concept of an upper-class group of women managing their own labor did not exist.

When Woodrow Wilson spoke of the free enterprise system as the most effective economic system, he was specifically referring to the liberal concept of the economic market. According to this principle, maximum freedom leads to maximum _____ our openness being the benchmark for our stability.

16

Which choice completes the text so that it conforms to the conventions of Standard English?

(A) productivity with

(B) productivity, with

(C) productivity; with

(D) productivity. With

For a long time, civil rights activists have been vociferous in their assertion that one of the primary reasons why Blacks, Hispanics, and other minority groups have encountered significant obstacles in establishing themselves in the business world _____ that they lack access to the vast orders and subcontracts that large companies typically generate.

17

Which choice completes the text so that it conforms to the conventions of Standard English?

(A) is

(B) are

(C) have been

(D) were

Henry IV was a pivotal figure in the history of France, credited with ending the turbulent Wars of Religion and laying the groundwork for the absolutist monarchy that would follow. His reign was characterized by a pragmatic approach to governance, as he sought to balance the competing interests of the nobility and the ordinary people. Despite facing significant challenges throughout his reign, _____

18

Which choice completes the text so that it conforms to the conventions of Standard English?

(A) the direction of French history was influenced by the leadership and vision of Henry IV, which also laid the groundwork for establishing a powerful centralized state.

(B) the establishment of a strong and centralized state was made possible through the leadership and vision of Henry IV, which also contributed to shaping the trajectory of French history.

(C) Henry IV's leadership and vision helped shape the course of French history and establish a strong centralized state.

(D) the course of French history was shaped, and the leadership and vision of Henry IV established the foundations of a strong centralized state.

Section 1, Module 2: Reading and Writing

Directions ⌄

32:00
Hide

Annotate

More

Material ecology is a multidisciplinary field that explores the relationships between materials, the environment, and human society. Material ecology has significant applications in areas such as architecture, product design, and _____ has the potential to revolutionize the way we approach resource management and environmental stewardship.

19

Which choice completes the text so that it conforms to the conventions of Standard English?

(A) manufacturing

(B) manufacturing and

(C) manufacturing, and

(D) manufacturing; and

Section 1, Module 2: Reading and Writing

Directions ⌄

32:00
Hide

Annotate

More

Many research studies have been conducted on various aspects of the Moon, including its formation, geology, and potential for future exploration and colonization. Some research methods used to study the Moon _____ remote sensing from orbiting spacecraft, a sample analysis of lunar rocks and soil, and computer modeling of its evolution and surface features.

20

Which choice completes the text so that it conforms to the conventions of Standard English?

(A) include

(B) including

(C) to include

(D) having included

Despite its status as a ground-breaking movement, Impressionism can trace its origins to earlier painting _____ as Naturalism and Realism, which were already questioning conventional views of aesthetic beauty and the artist's connection with the state.

21

Which choice completes the text so that it conforms to the conventions of Standard English?

- (A) forms such
- (B) forms, such
- (C) forms; such
- (D) forms: such

In 1955, McNeil Laboratories created Tylenol, a popular pain reliever and fever reducer. The development process included crucial steps such as synthesizing _____ tests to ensure safety and efficacy; and designing user-friendly packaging. Tylenol has since become a common household item, offering relief for headaches, muscle aches, and various other ailments.

22

Which choice completes the text so that it conforms to the conventions of Standard English?

- (A) acetaminophen; the active ingredient conducting
- (B) acetaminophen, the active ingredient; conducting
- (C) acetaminophen, the active ingredient, conducting
- (D) acetaminophen, the active ingredient conducting;

From the rise of televised sports in the 1950s to the explosion of digital media in the 21st century, sports coverage has become a global industry, generating billions of dollars in revenue and shaping the public's perception of what it means to be an athlete. _____ this increased visibility has also led to debates about the commodification of athletes, the exploitation of amateur athletes, and the impact of sports on society.

23

Which choice completes the text with the most logical transition?

- (A) However,
- (B) For instance,
- (C) Consequently,
- (D) Similarly,

Public-awareness campaigns are designed to inform and educate the public on critical social issues and health-related topics. These campaigns typically use a variety of media to reach a broad audience. They often rely on persuasive messaging and emotional appeals to motivate people to take action or change their behavior. The effectiveness of public-awareness campaigns can take time to measure. _____ they have the potential to influence attitudes and behaviors on a large scale, making them a valuable tool in promoting social change.

24

Which choice completes the text with the most logical transition?

- (A) Consequently,
- (B) For instance,
- (C) Still,
- (D) Similarly,

The Twentieth Amendment to the United States Constitution, ratified in 1933, sets a date for the inauguration of the President and Vice President and establishes procedures for situations in which there is no President-elect. _____ it sets a date for the beginning of sessions of Congress, ensuring that there is no gap in the continuity of government. The amendment's goal was to shorten the time between the election and the start of a new administration, providing for a more efficient transition of power.

25

Which choice completes the text with the most logical transition?

- (A) Specifically,
- (B) Thus,
- (C) Regardless,
- (D) Similarly,

"*The Joys of Motherhood*" by Buchi Emecheta is a thought-provoking novel that explores the complexities of motherhood in a patriarchal society. Set in colonial Nigeria, the story follows the life of Nnu Ego, a woman who desires nothing more than to become a mother. _____ the harsh realities of motherhood quickly set in as she struggles to provide for her children and maintain her dignity in a society that devalues women.

26

Which choice completes the text with the most logical transition?

- (A) However,
- (B) Furthermore,
- (C) Thus,
- (D) Likewise,

Section 1, Module 2: Reading and Writing
Directions ⌄

32:00
Hide

✎
Annotate

⋮
More

While researching a topic, a student has taken the following notes:

- John Friedman is an American economist known for researching income inequality, intergenerational mobility, and public policy.
- His innovative methods have led to a deeper understanding of the complex factors contributing to economic disparities and social mobility.
- Friedman's research has informed local, state, and federal policy initiatives.
- He is widely recognized as a thought leader and has earned numerous awards and honors for his economics and social policy contributions.

27

The student wants to emphasize the significance of the methods John Friedman employed. Which choice most effectively uses relevant information from the notes to accomplish this goal?

(A) The outcomes of Friedman's research have influenced policy decisions and actions at various levels of governance, including those at the local, state, and federal levels.

(B) He is widely acknowledged as an influential thinker and has received many accolades and distinctions for his contributions to economics and social policy.

(C) His unique methods have resulted in a more profound comprehension of the intricate elements that give rise to economic inequalities and social mobility.

(D) John Friedman is an economist from the United States who is recognized for studying income inequality, social mobility across generations, and public policy.

IV

TEST 4 Module 1		
No.	Answer	Question Type
1	D	Text Completion
2	A	Text Completion
3	B	Text Completion
4	D	Text Completion
5	A	Function
6	D	Direct Comprehension / Poem
7	A	Main Purpose
8	D	Main Idea / Poem
9	C	Cross-Text
10	A	Command of Evidence / Quantitative
11	A	Command of Evidence / Literature
12	B	Command of Evidence / Textual
13	B	Inference
14	C	Inference
15	B	Conventions of Standard English
16	A	Conventions of Standard English
17	C	Conventions of Standard English
18	C	Conventions of Standard English
19	B	Conventions of Standard English
20	D	Conventions of Standard English
21	B	Conventions of Standard English
22	C	Conventions of Standard English
23	D	Transition
24	B	Transition
25	C	Transition
26	D	Transition
27	D	Note Summary

TEST 4 Module 2		
No.	Answer	Question Type
1	A	Text Completion
2	D	Text Completion
3	D	Text Completion
4	B	Text Completion
5	A	Vocabulary in Context
6	B	Main Purpose / Poem
7	C	Structure / Poem
8	A	Function
9	D	Cross-Text
10	C	Main Idea
11	A	Command of Evidence / Textual
12	A	Command of Evidence / Quantitative
13	C	Command of Evidence / Literature
14	D	Command of Evidence / Textual
15	D	Inference
16	B	Conventions of Standard English
17	A	Conventions of Standard English
18	C	Conventions of Standard English
19	B	Conventions of Standard English
20	A	Conventions of Standard English
21	A	Conventions of Standard English
22	B	Conventions of Standard English
23	A	Transition
24	C	Transition
25	D	Transition
26	A	Transition
27	C	Note Summary

DIGITAL SAT Advanced SCORING CHART

Raw score to Score Conversion Chart

Raw Score	Score	Incorrect	Score
54	800	26	530
53	770	25	530
52	740	24	510
51	730	23	510
50	710	22	490
49	710	21	480
48	690	20	480
47	680	19	460
46	680	18	450
45	670	17	430
44	660	16	400
43	650	15	380
42	630	14	360
41	630	13	340
40	620	12	330
39	620	11	310
38	620	10	300
37	610	9	280
36	600	8	260
35	600	7	260
34	590	6	250
33	590	5	240
32	580	4	220
31	580	3	200
30	570	2	200
29	560	1	200
28	550	0	200
27	540		

Digital SAT
Practice Test #V

The questions in this section address a number of important reading and writing skills. Each question includes one or more passages, which may include a table or graph. Read each passage and question carefully, and then choose the best answer to the question based on the text(s).

All questions in this section are multiple-choice with four answer choices. Each question has a single best answer.

Section 1, Module 1: Reading and Writing

For young children, learning a language is almost instinctive: Children have a _____ ability to absorb information and develop language skills quickly, as their brains are more flexible and receptive to new information, which makes them more open to adopting the new language's sounds, vocabulary, and grammar rules.

1

Which choice completes the text with the most logical and precise word or phrase?

(A) remarkable

(B) natural

(C) proven

(D) limited

Section 1, Module 1: Reading and Writing

Ants of the genus Solenopsis exhibit _____ behavior, working together in colonies to build intricate nests and care for their young. However, unlike other communal insects, these ants are capable of stinging, which can be painful or even life-threatening to humans and other animals.

2

Which choice completes the text with the most logical and precise word or phrase?

(A) social

(B) deviant

(C) aggressive

(D) disruptive

Section 1, Module 1: Reading and Writing

Directions ∨

32:00
Hide

Annotate More

A trade war can have negative impacts on the economies of the countries directly involved in the war as well as on the global economy as a whole. The _____ of tariffs on imported goods can result in decreased trade, reduced investment, and increased inflation, leading to higher prices for consumers, lower profits for businesses, and overall economic instability.

3

Which choice completes the text with the most logical and precise word or phrase?

(A) deduction

(B) nullification

(C) imposition

(D) reclamation

SCORE SHAKE

Question 3 of 27 ∧

Back   Next

Section 1, Module 1: Reading and Writing

Directions ∨

32:00
Hide

Annotate More

The enigmatic entity at the heart of our galaxy, some 26,000 light-years away from our planet, Sagittarius A*, boasts a _____ mass of approximately four million solar masses. As the primary gravitational driver in the galactic center, this black hole exerts a significant influence on the motion of the stars within the Milky Way.

4

Which choice completes the text with the most logical and precise word or phrase?

(A) colossal

(B) resplendent

(C) tangled

(D) repugnant

SCORE SHAKE

Question 4 of 27 ∧

Back   Next

The findings of a study published in the Journal of Health Psychology in 2019 showed that Chinese immigrants living in the United States who practiced traditional Chinese medicine had significantly lower levels of depression and anxiety than those who did not. The study, which used a survey-based methodology to collect data from over 500 Chinese immigrants, provides evidence that cultural practices and beliefs can have a positive impact on mental health. The results suggest that traditional Chinese medicine may be an effective way to promote mental health in this population.

5

Which choice best states the main purpose of the text?

(A) To prove that traditional Chinese medicine is more effective than modern Western medicine in treating mental health issues

(B) To explore the relationship between traditional Chinese medicine and mental health among Chinese immigrants in the United States

(C) To argue that only Chinese immigrants in the United States should use traditional Chinese medicine for their mental health

(D) To suggest that the results of the study can be applied to all cultural groups, regardless of their specific beliefs and practices

SCORE SHAKE

Question 5 of 27 ⌃

Back   Next

The following text is from Ellis Parker Butler's poem *A Culinary Puzzle*. The word "tasks" is used here to mean "asks."

In our dainty little kitchen,
Where my aproned wife is queen
Over all the tin-pan people,
In a realm exceeding clean,
Oft I like to loiter, watching
While she mixes things for tea;
And she tasks me, slyly smiling,
"Now just guess what this will be!"

Little fraud! she never tells me
Until 'tis baked and browned
And I think I know the reason
For her secrecy profound
She herself with all her fine airs
And her books on cookery,
Could not answer, should I ask her,
"Dearest, what will that mess be?"

6

Which choice best states the main idea of the text?

(A) The speaker is more concerned with watching his wife than answering her question.

(B) The speaker believes that his wife is a messy cook.

(C) The speaker's wife does not herself know what she is preparing.

(D) The speaker cannot understand the reason for his wife's secrecy.

SCORE SHAKE

Question 6 of 27 ⌃

Back   Next

Section 1, Module 1: Reading and Writing

32:00
Hide

Annotate

More

Directions ⌄

A study published in the journal Sex Roles asked over 500 participants to rate their level of agreement with statements such as "I believe that men and women should have equal rights" and "I believe that men and women should have different roles in society." The results showed that gender roles are not as fixed as previously thought. This finding suggests that gender roles are more fluid and that we should not make assumptions about someone's gender based on their appearance or behavior.

7

Which choice best states the main idea of the text?

(A) The study suggests that people should not make any assumptions about someone's gender at all.

(B) The study surveyed 500 participants, which is not enough to represent the entire population.

(C) One should avoid presuming an individual's gender solely on the basis of their looks or actions.

(D) Gender roles are non-existent since they change over time.

Section 1, Module 1: Reading and Writing

32:00
Hide

Annotate

More

Directions ⌄

Concealed beneath 2.5 miles of ice, Lake Vostok has piqued the interest of researchers. Its deposits contain a distinct record of Antarctica's climate and the potential for ancient life forms to exist in its depths. International groups of scientists are urging their governments to fund a costly, long-term exploration project. If successful, <u>new facilities will be established, logistical networks developed, aircraft will deliver vast amounts of fuel, and remotely operated autonomous deep-diving robots will be deployed into the lake's waters via boreholes</u>. Despite the considerable challenges and potential impact on the lake, unveiling its mysteries could significantly advance Antarctic science.

8

Which choice best describes the function of the underlined portion in the text as a whole?

(A) It highlights the costs associated with scientific exploration.

(B) It conveys the excitement of researchers over a groundbreaking advancement.

(C) It signifies the difficulty of successfully completing a project.

(D) It underscores the magnitude of the suggested undertaking.

Section 1, Module 1: Reading and Writing

Annotate   More

The Axolotl (*Ambystoma mexicanum*), a fascinating member of the *Ambystomatidae* family, possesses an extraordinary ability to regenerate its body parts. Native to Mexico, this peculiar salamander can regrow lost limbs, spinal cord, heart, and even parts of its brain, making it a captivating subject for researchers studying regeneration. Axolotl's unique talent for healing itself without scarring has positioned it as an invaluable model organism in the world of science, offering potential insights into human regenerative medicine and tissue repair.

9

According to the text, which aspect of Axolotl's regenerative capabilities is most closely linked to its significance in scientific research?

(A) The Axolotl's extraordinary ability to produce supplementary limbs, spinal cord, heart, and sections of its brain as reserve organs

(B) That Axolotl originates from the country of Mexico where scientific investigation can be carried out with relatively fewer regulatory limitations

(C) The Axolotl's exceptional skill of healing itself without leaving any scars behind

(D) Its classification as a member of the *Ambystomatidae* family within the animal kingdom

SCORE SHAKE

Back   Next

Section 1, Module 1: Reading and Writing

Annotate   More

Text 1
Professional dental and medical organizations have repeatedly confirmed the effectiveness and safety of fluoridation, a process of adding controlled amounts of fluoride to public water supplies to minimize tooth decay.

Text 2
During a public meeting on October 17, 2009, in Yellow Springs, Ohio, where the possibility of ending a fluoridation program was being discussed, Paul Connett presented the scientific arguments against the practice. Following responses from a county health commissioner and local dentists, a <u>participant</u> in the audience advocated for the right to choose what substances to ingest, stating that she should have the freedom to choose, rather than having the decision being made for her by a government agency.

10

Based on the texts, how does the "participant" mentioned in Text 2 respond to the idea introduced in Text 1?

(A) By exploring the ethical consequences of a practice discussed in Text 1

(B) By providing further details about an argument mentioned in Text 1

(C) By endorsing the philosophical stance articulated in Text 1

(D) By calling into question the credibility of the evidence presented in Text 1

SCORE SHAKE

Back   Next

Section 1, Module 1: Reading and Writing

Directions ⌄

32:00
Hide

Annotate   More

The following text is excerpted from a novel describing the author's memory of a childhood experience. He remembers how he reacted to a fearful situation while a student in the New York City public school system during the late 1930s. In the novel, a taller classmate named "McCahty" gives the author an Indian club, a wooden club used in exercise and juggling, because the author was not tall enough to reach the club: _____.

11

Which quotation from the text most effectively illustrates the claim?

(A) "I remember thinking that if McCahty were to use one of those clubs to attack me, I would be entirely at his mercy. I was certain I had only one hope: to attack him first."

(B) "I made a grab for a club, but, as I was so much smaller than the other boys, the clubs were out of reach."

(C) "With fear trumping prudence, I swung the club as high as I could to hit McCahty in the back of the head."

(D) "I don't know what he saw as he looked at me, but his eyes became quizzical as if he couldn't believe that I really existed. His stare softened and his mouth did something of which I had never imagined it was capable."

Reef Herbivore Mass

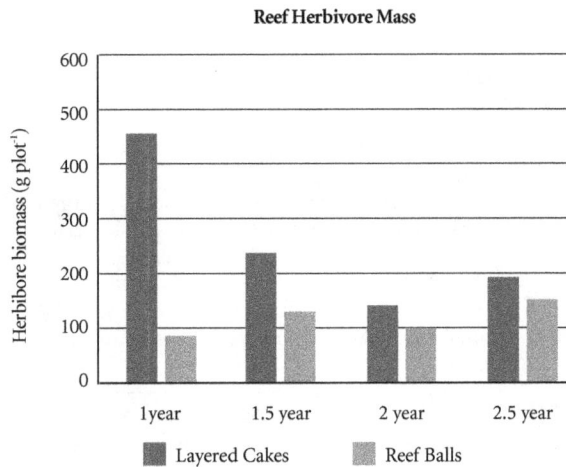

Diving beneath the surface of a vibrant, underwater world, we encounter a diverse ecosystem thriving on artificial reefs. The number, biomass, and composition of fish assemblages on various artificial reef types can vary substantially, with some coral types supporting almost five times as many herbivores as others. In this study, Alwin Hylkema et al. compared the fish assemblage on two artificial reef types: reef balls and layered cakes. The reef balls were domes with a single void space with multiple holes, while the layered cakes had different layers of concrete with multiple contiguous shelters in between. Although layered cakes initially harbored vastly higher herbivorous fish biomass, this effect was lost during consecutive monitoring events. This seems to be the result of the higher territorial fish abundance around the layered cakes where almost four times more chasing behavior was recorded compared to the reef balls.

12

Which choice best describes the data in the graph that supports the study's findings?

(A) In year 1, the herbivore biomass per plot was less than 100g for the reef balls, but it gradually increased to 150g per plot by year 2.5.

(B) The herbivore biomass per plot was just under 500g in year 1 for the reef balls, and it remained at that level until year 2.5.

(C) In year 1, the herbivore biomass per plot was approximately 460g for the layered cakes, but it precipitously dropped to just over 200g per plot by year 1.5.

(D) The herbivore biomass per plot was just under 100g in year 1 for the reef balls, and approximately 460g for the layered cakes.

Section 1, Module 1: Reading and Writing

Directions ∨

32:00

Hide

✎ Annotate

⋮ More

Medical anthropology is a field of study that examines the cultural and biological aspects of health and illness. A recent study conducted by the University of California, San Francisco, found that medical anthropology can help to identify and address health disparities among different populations. The research analyzed the experiences of individuals from different cultural backgrounds and found that cultural beliefs, values, and practices can have a significant impact on health outcomes. This suggests that medical anthropology can be used to better understand and address health disparities.

13

Which statement, if true, would most directly support the researchers' claim?

(A) The study demonstrated that incorporating an understanding of cultural and social factors in healthcare interventions can improve health outcomes in diverse populations by 70% compared to traditional medical approaches.

(B) The study showed that the majority of participants preferred to receive medical care from providers who had cultural competence training.

(C) The University of California, San Francisco, has a diverse student body, with more than 20% of students identifying as multicultural.

(D) The research analyzed the experiences of individuals from different cultural backgrounds and found that religious faith has a significantly greater impact on health outcomes than do cultural beliefs and practices.

Small island nations, particularly those located in developing regions, are especially susceptible to the effects of climate change. It is notable that in many of these island nations, environmental conditions and cultural traditions are deeply intertwined, making the impact of climate change more severe. The ramifications of climate change can be particularly acute for regions that are heavily reliant on hydroelectric power, as reduced water availability can significantly affect this power source. Additionally, an increase in temperatures and climate-related disasters, such as sea-level rise, salt-water intrusion, and crop failure, would trigger economic stresses and social conflicts that could exacerbate armed conflicts. While some experts have suggested reinforcing infrastructure as a potential solution, others caution that it may not be a practical long-term solution. The information about the social and economic effects of climate change suggests that _____

14

Which choice most logically completes the text?

(A) social tensions and armed conflicts will make the reinforcement of the infrastructure of island nations impractical.

(B) the culture of some nations will be more substantially affected than others by climate change.

(C) people with fewer economic resources typically have a culture that is particularly tied to their environment.

(D) the use of hydroelectric power will decrease on small island nations as climate change worsens.

For as long as Harvey Houses, a chain of restaurants, served rail travelers through the mid-twentieth century, working there was a steady and lucrative position for women. Living independently and demonstrating intense work _____ the Harvey Girls became a transformative force in the American West.

15

Which choice completes the text so that it conforms to the conventions of Standard English?

(A) ethic;

(B) ethic:

(C) ethic, and

(D) ethic,

The fact that Dr. Morgenthaler's most recent observation was made with largely accessible instruments _____ the possibility of more studies, similar and different, in kind. "The more monitoring we can get, the better it will be," said Dr. Davies.

16

Which choice completes the text so that it conforms to the conventions of Standard English?

- (A) open
- (B) opens
- (C) have opened
- (D) are opening

Caspar David Friedrich, one of the most prominent German artists of the 18th and 19th centuries, is recognized for his ability to produce beautiful landscapes. *Evening Landscape with Two Men* is one of the _____ most famous sunset artworks. This piece, created in the Romantic style, depicts two men, maybe brothers, dressed in hats and long robes staring at the sunset with their backs to the viewer.

17

Which choice completes the text so that it conforms to the conventions of Standard English?

- (A) artists
- (B) artist's
- (C) artists'
- (D) artist of

In an intriguing social science experiment, researchers observed participants' behavior within an artificially constructed society. By manipulating cultural _____ unveiled the elasticity of human adaptability, shedding light on our innate ability to conform and resist in response to diverse social pressures.

18

Which choice completes the text so that it conforms to the conventions of Standard English?

- (A) norms and expectations; they
- (B) norms, and expectations, they
- (C) norms and expectations, they
- (D) norms and expectations they

Sugar can have detrimental effects on our health. It can contribute to obesity and tooth decay; additionally, it increases the risk of type 2 diabetes and heart disease. By fueling inflammation and impairing the body's ability to regulate insulin, _____.

19

Which choice completes the text so that it conforms to the conventions of Standard English?

- (A) excessive sugar intake wreaks havoc on our wellbeing
- (B) our wellbeing is devastated by excessive sugar intake
- (C) the damage we suffer from excessive sugar intake can be significant
- (D) we can be severely harmed by excessive sugar intake

Better than soil at holding moisture, compost (organic matter such as food scraps and yard debris) minimizes water waste and storm runoff, _____ on watering costs, and helps reduce erosion on embankments near bodies of water.

20

Which choice completes the text so that it conforms to the conventions of Standard English?

- (A) it increases savings
- (B) savings increase
- (C) increases savings
- (D) also it increases savings

Augustus, also known as Octavian, was the first Roman emperor who ruled from 27 BC until he died in AD 14. During his reign, Augustus implemented numerous reforms, including establishing a stable and efficient government, expanding the empire's boundaries, and creating a lasting legacy. _____ his influence can be seen in the art, architecture, and literature of the time, shaping the course of Western civilization for centuries to come.

21

Which choice completes the text with the most logical transition?

- (A) However,
- (B) In addition,
- (C) Consequently,
- (D) For example,

Because elephant groups frequently break up and reunite, reunions hold greater significance in elephant society than among primates. Typically, elephants greet each other by reaching their trunks into each other's mouths, a gesture perhaps equivalent to a human peck on the cheek. _____ after extended absences, members of family and bond groups greet one another with remarkably theatrical displays. The fact that the intensity of these reunions reflects both the duration of separation and the level of intimacy suggests that elephants possess a keen sense of alienation and reunion.

22

Which choice completes the text with the most logical transition?

(A) However,

(B) In addition,

(C) Consequently,

(D) For example,

A magnificent sunset is among the most stunning views one can witness. The blending of hues at dusk can be tranquil and soothing, with warm yellows, vivid reds, and flaming oranges capturing the eye's attention and comforting the spirit. _____ it comes as no surprise that numerous famous sunset paintings have been created to transfer this breathtaking experience onto the canvas.

23

Which choice completes the text with the most logical transition?

(A) To wit,

(B) Namely,

(C) Therfore,

(D) For example,

There are significant differences in how mothers and fathers describe their parenting styles. For example, about half of mothers (51%) say they tend to be overprotective, compared to 38% of fathers. _____, fathers (24%) are more likely than mothers (16%) to say they tend to give their children too much freedom.

24

Which choice completes the text with the most logical transition?

- Ⓐ As a result,
- Ⓑ Conversely,
- Ⓒ To illustrate,
- Ⓓ At any rate,

While researching a topic, a student has taken the following notes:

- Ghibli Park is a theme park in Japan that features attractions based on some of the movies produced by Studio Ghibli.
- Studio Ghibli is known for animated movies, particularly the ones featuring the work of director, author, and animator Hayao Miyazaki.
- The park has five themed areas, each based on a different Ghibli movie.
- There is a railway station at the park entrance but, surprisingly, no parking lot in the park itself.
- It is located within a larger park, and no trees were cut down to accommodate it.
- It has no large rides like a typical theme park.

25

The student wants to emphasize the uniqueness of Ghibli Park. Which choice most effectively uses relevant information from the notes to accomplish this goal?

- Ⓐ Ghibli Park is a theme park in Japan that is located within a larger park.
- Ⓑ The park has no parking lot and no large rides.
- Ⓒ There is a railway station at the entrance to the park, which features five themed areas.
- Ⓓ Hayao Miyazaki is the director, author, and animator responsible for some of Studio Ghibli's best known movies.

Section 1, Module 1: Reading and Writing

32:00
Hide

Annotate   More

While researching a topic, a student has taken the following notes:

- A weed is any plant that is undesirable in a certain context, especially if it interferes with the growth of desirable plants.
- Certain types of weeds, called ruderals, have advantages that allow them to dominate in areas where the soil has been damaged or disturbed.
- Sometimes weeds dominate an environment that they are new to because the animals and plants that typically compete with them are not present.
- This is called the "natural enemies hypothesis."
- The Klamath weed threatened millions of hectares of grain and grazing land in North America until its natural "enemies" were imported to the area.
- Even a plant that does not harm others can be considered a weed if it harbors pests that attack other plants.

26

The student wants to explain and provide an example of how weeds can dominate an environment. Which choice most effectively uses relevant information from the notes to accomplish this goal?

(A) A plant that is undesirable in a certain context, such as a ruderal, can have advantages that allows it to dominate in areas where the soil has been damaged or disturbed.

(B) A plant can be considered a weed if it lacks natural enemies or because it harbors pests that attack other plants.

(C) The Klamath weed, which interfered with the growth of desirable plants, threatened millions of hectares of grain and grazing land in North America

(D) Weeds, such as the Klamath weed in North America, threaten other plants because the animals and plants that typically compete with the weed are not present.

While researching a topic, a student has taken the following notes:

- Postmodern architecture, which began in the 1960s, was in part a reaction against a perceived lack of variety in architectural styles of that time.
- Postmodern architects often used several apparently contrasting styles in their designs.
- The idea that "less is more" was a principle that many postmodernists believed was too rigid.
- Some buildings designed in the postmodern style incorporated elements from different time periods in a way that was meant to be somewhat humorous.
- The Sydney Opera House in Australia is perhaps the best-known example of postmodern architecture.

27

The student wants to convey some of the elements of postmodern architecture. Which choice most effectively uses relevant information from the notes to accomplish this goal?

(A) The postmodern architecture of the 1960s led to the design of the Sydney Opera House, completed in 1973.

(B) The idea that "less is more" was popular idea among many architects prior to the advent of postmodernism.

(C) A building designed in the postmodern style could combine elements from different time periods in a humorous way.

(D) Some architects in the 1960s designed buildings in part because of what they considered to be a lack of variety in architectural styles.

Practice Test Break

You can resume this practice test as soon as you're ready to move on. On test day, you'll wait until the clock counts down.

Take a Break

You may leave the room, but do not disturb students who are still testing.

Do not exit the app or close your device.

Testing won't resume until you return.

Follow these rules during the break:

1. Do not access your phone, smartwatch, textbooks, notes, or the internet.

2. Do not eat or drink in the test room.

3. Do not speak in the test room; outside the test room, do not discuss the exam with anyone.

Remaing Break Time:

9:52

Resume Testing

The LGBTQ+ rights movement has had a profound effect on the visibility of LGBTQ+ individuals in art, allowing for a greater representation of _____ identities and catalyzing the emergence of these artists in the art world. This has opened up the art world to a more diverse range of perspectives, allowing for more inclusive and meaningful art to be created and appreciated.

1

Which choice completes the text with the most logical and precise word or phrase?

(A) eccentric

(B) outspoken

(C) queer

(D) whimsical

One of the most well-studied plants in plant genetics and genomics is *Arabidopsis thaliana*, which is widely used as a model organism for understanding the molecular mechanisms of plant growth. Research on *Arabidopsis thaliana* has been _____ gaining valuable insights into the genetic and genomic regulation of plants, contributing to the development of improved crop varieties and sustainable agriculture.

2

Which choice completes the text with the most logical and precise word or phrase?

(A) distant from

(B) conducive to

(C) tenacious in

(D) indolent in

A study published in 2020 identified a neural network in the prefrontal cortex that _____ risky decision-making. The study used a gambling task and neuroimaging to show that greater activity in this network was associated with more risk-taking behavior. The findings shed light on the underlying mechanisms of decision-making and could have implications for the treatment of conditions characterized by impulsivity and risk-taking.

3

Which choice completes the text with the most logical and precise word or phrase?

(A) proscribes

(B) consummates

(C) designates

(D) mediates

The pandemic caused a substantial decrease in consumer expenditure, which in turn had an unfavorable effect on small businesses. Many small enterprises had to shutter their operations permanently due to the pandemic, leading to a reduction in employment and economic activity in local communities. This has brought to the fore the requirement for efficacious governmental policies and support schemes to aid small businesses in _____ economic crises.

4

Which choice completes the text with the most logical and precise word or phrase?

(A) weathering

(B) defusing

(C) precipitating

(D) exacerbating

The following text is from Victor James Daley's poem *The Little People*. The word "contemn" means to treat with disrespect, and "weal" means "goodness."

Who are these strange small folk,
These that come to our homes as kings,
Asking nor leave nor grace,
Bending our necks to their yoke . . .?

Dimpled their hands and small,
Would ye, therefore, their might contemn?
Seem they for play designed?
Fate, and the Future withal,
Weal, yea and Woe, of mankind,
Lie hid in the palms of them.

These are the children dear,
From a country unknown of charts:
(Dim Land of Souls Unborn),
Rosy as morn they come here,
Filling with joy forlorn
Waste places in our hearts.

5

Which choice best describes the function of the underlined portion in the text as a whole?

- (A) It reveals that the "*Little People*" of the title refers to children.
- (B) It is a response to someone who would say "yes" to the questions in the same stanza.
- (C) It is a criticism of children who act in the manner described in the first stanza.
- (D) It is an answer to the question posed in the first stanza.

The following text is from Walter DeLa Mare's poem *All But Blind*. The speaker refers to three kinds of animals in the text (besides worms).

All but blind
  In his chambered hole
Gropes for worms
  The four-clawed Mole.

All but blind
  n the evening sky
The hooded Bat
  Twirls softly by.

All but blind
  In the burning day
The Barn-Owl blunders
  On her way.

And blind as are
  These three to me,
So, blind to Some-one
  I must be.

6

Which choice best states the main idea of the text?

- (A) Moles, bats, and barn-owls might seem blind, but they can see things that people cannot.
- (B) Perfect sight is impossible for both people and animals.
- (C) Even animals with limited sight have an understanding of the natural world that can be compared with human understanding.
- (D) Others regard the speaker as ignorant in a way comparable to how people view animals with limited sight.

Section 1, Module 2: Reading and Writing
Directions ⌄

32:00
Hide

Annotate   More

A recent study published in the journal *Nature Climate Change* unveiled a disconcerting trend in global environmental and ecological concerns. Investigating the repercussions of climate change on global ecosystems, the study's authors discovered an alarming acceleration in the rate of species extinction. Findings revealed a staggering 50% increase in extinction since the 1970s, with tropical regions bearing the brunt of the losses. These results underscore the significant influence of climate change on global ecosystems, necessitating prompt and decisive action to shield species from extinction. The study not only emphasizes the importance of further probing the ramifications of climate change on species but also demands the execution of measures to mitigate climate change's impact on global ecosystems.

7

Which choice best states the main idea of the study?

(A) The surge in species extinction rates, particularly in tropical regions, is due to the substantial influence of climate change and needs to be addressed.

(B) Since the 1970s, a staggering increase of over 50% in the rate of species extinction has been observed, signaling a concerning trend in global biodiversity.

(C) Decisive actions that have mitigated climate change's impact have shielded many species from extinction.

(D) Finding methods to lessen the impact of climate change is of greater importance than continuing to probe the ramifications of climate change.

Section 1, Module 2: Reading and Writing
Directions ⌄

32:00
Hide

Annotate   More

This text is from Mary Shelly, *Frankenstein* originally published in 1818.

"For some days I haunted the spot where these scenes had taken place; sometimes wishing to see you, sometimes resolved to quit the world and its miseries forever. At length I wandered towards these mountains, and have <u>ranged</u> through their immense recesses, consumed by a burning passion which you alone can gratify. We may not part until you have promised to comply with my requisition."

8

As used in the text, what does the word "ranged" most nearly mean?

(A) fluctuated

(B) aligned

(C) bracketed

(D) roamed

Section 1, Module 2: Reading and Writing

Directions ∨

32:00

Hide

Annotate More

Text 1

The comparative benefits of robotic spaceflight over human spaceflight are not up for debate: not only is robotic spaceflight more affordable and safer, it is also scientifically more productive. However, while rovers represent an incredible technological feat, they lack the human element that generates drama and that captures our imagination. Human spaceflight is truly awe-inspiring, representing the very best of humanity's aspirations and capabilities.

Text 2

Inspired by the impressive accomplishments of Apollo astronauts, advocates of human spaceflight continue to argue that programs that incorporate people and machines are more effective than those relying on robots alone. However, the exorbitant costs associated with transporting humans through space have given pause to this idea. When it comes to the future of human space travel, the cost is the single most inhibiting factor.

9

Based on the texts, how would the author of Text 1 respond to the argument made in Text 2?

(A) By recognizing the efficacy of space operations that combine human labor with technological innovation

(B) By making the argument that human space missions provide non-material advantages that transcend any financial constraints

(C) By denouncing unfeasible proposals that impose a significant financial burden on taxpayers for space mission operations

(D) By rejecting the notion that robotic spaceflight is merely a byproduct of the hard work and achievements of past generations

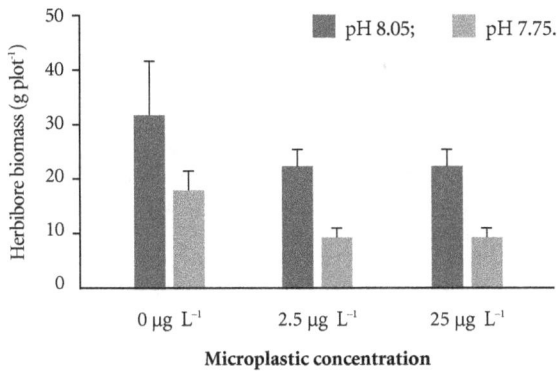

Herbibore biomass (g plot⁻¹) vs Microplastic concentration, with legend pH 8.05; pH 7.75.

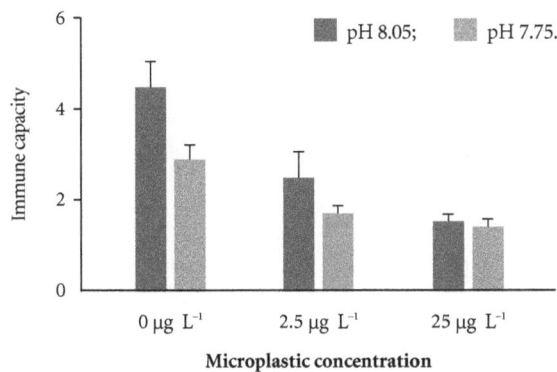

Immune capacity vs Microplastic concentration, with legend pH 8.05; pH 7.75.

Xizhi Huang et al. evaluated the potential impact of ocean acidification and microplastics on the health of a mussel species, *Mytilus coruscus*. They examined the mussel's immunity and byssus properties. Byssus threads are support structures produced by many bivalves including mussels. These are strong, silky fibers used to anchor themselves to surfaces in their environment. However, byssus production demands a lot of energy. In energy-limiting conditions, the quality of byssus threads can suffer. When immunity needs to be strengthened against pathogens, energy devoted to byssus formation would be further diminished. The researchers theorized that the predicted increase in ocean acidity (pH 7.75) from the current pH 8.05, as well as the increased concentration of microplastics in future oceans, would lead to impairment in immunity and byssus production.

10

Which choice best describes the data from the graph that best supports Xizhi Huang and the team's theory?

(A) The increase in acidity from pH 8.05 to 7.75 decreases the immune capacity of mussels but increases their byssus thread production regardless of microplastic concentration.

(B) The increase in microplastic concentration from 0 to 25 µg/l is directly proportional to the immune capacity and byssus thread production of mussels.

(C) The immune capacities of mussels at 25 µg/l microplastic concentration largely decreases when acidity decreases from pH 7.75 to pH 8.05.

(D) The increase in acidity from pH 8.05 to 7.75 and the increase of microplastic concentration from 0 to 25 µg/l result in a decrease in the immune capacity of mussels and their byssus thread production.

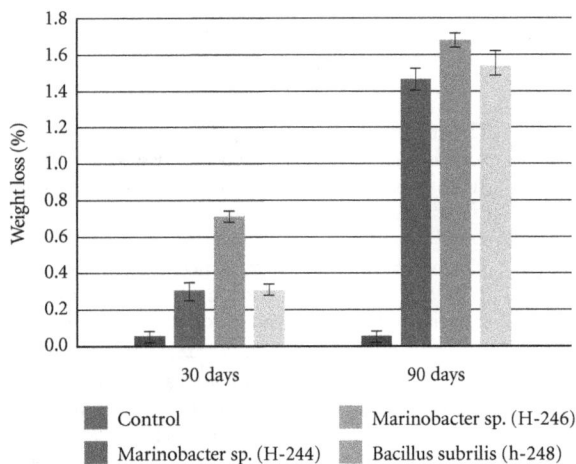

Control

Marinobacter sp. (H-244)

Marinobacter sp. (H-246)

Bacillus subrilis (h-248)

In today's world, polyethylene is used in many aspects of daily life. But without any safe and appropriate disposal option, its excessive use resulted in ocean accumulation ultimately causing marine pollution. One of the most effective ways to manage this kind of pollution from synthetic plastic waste is through biodegradation by marine bacteria. In the present study, Shrikant Khandare et al. exposed a low-density polyethylene (LDPE) film to three marine bacterial isolates, Marinobacter sp. H-244 and Marinobacter sp. H-246 and Bacillus subtilis H-248, for 30 and 90 days to allow biodegradation to occur. The researchers claim that the reduction in the weight of the LDPE film shows that the microbes utilized the carbon in the material as a food source and consequently reduced the weight of the LDPE film.

11

Which choice best describes the data from the graph that supports the researcher's claim?

(A) The percent weight loss of the H-244 and H-248 samples were the same in both the 30 day and 90 day treatment.

(B) Significant weight loss of the LDPE film was seen in the 90-day treatment (1.46%, 1.68% and 1.54%) for all three marine bacterial isolates relative to the control flask.

(C) The amount of LDPE in the control sample did not show any change after 90 days.

(D) H-246 showed the largest biodegradation rate of LDPE in both the 30-day and 90-day treatment relative to H-244 and H-248.

Eating a healthy diet is an important part of maintaining a healthy lifestyle. A recent study published in Nutrients looked at the impact of a Mediterranean diet on cardiovascular health. The study included 1,500 individuals and tracked their dietary intake over a five-year period. The results showed that those who followed a Mediterranean diet had a 17% lower risk of developing cardiovascular disease than those who did not. Additionally, the Mediterranean diet was associated with a lower risk of stroke and hypertension. These findings suggest that following a Mediterranean diet may be beneficial for cardiovascular health and overall well-being.

12

Which choice best states the main idea of the study?

(A) Some participants who followed a Mediterranean diet scored high on the obesity index.

(B) Olive oil, which is commonly used in Mediterranean cuisine, is known to promote reduced inflammation and enhanced cognitive function.

(C) 17% of the 1,500 participants were diagnosed with cardiovascular disease after consuming the Mediterranean diet for five years.
Mediterranean diet for five years.

(D) Participants who followed the Mediterranean diet reported higher levels of physical activity than the control group.

Section 1, Module 2: Reading and Writing
Directions ⌄

32:00
Hide

✎
Annotate

⋮
More

Shirley, A Tale is a social novel by the English novelist Charlotte Brontë, first published in 1849. In the novel, Shirley Keeldar, a young woman of twenty-one who has inherited a fortune and land in Yorkshire, England regards love as an essential requirement for a fulfilling marriage: _____

13

Which quotation from *Shirley, A Tale* most effectively illustrates the claim?

(A) "And I ask in what sense that young man is worthy of me?"
"He has twice your money,—twice your common sense;—equal connections,—equal respectability."
"Had he my money counted five score times, I would take no vow to love him."

(B) "That conduct alone sinks him in a gulf of immeasurable inferiority. His intellect reaches no standard I can esteem— there is a second stumbling block. His views are narrow; his feelings are blunt; his tastes are coarse; his manners vulgar."

(C) "Take care, madam!"
"Scrupulous care I will take, Mr. Sympson. Before I marry, I am resolved to esteem—to admire—to love."
"Preposterous stuff! indecorous! unwomanly!"

(D) "And if this love of yours should fall on a beggar?"
"On a beggar it will never fall. Mendicancy is not estimable."

Different factors influence the longevity of certain cultural traditions. Researchers of a study published in the journal *Evolution and Human Behavior* claim that traditions that require more investment cost in terms of time, money, or effort are more likely to persist over time. This could be due to the fact that these traditions are seen as more meaningful and valuable to individuals and communities who practice them. As such, they are more likely to be passed down from one generation to the next. This hypothesis was tested by asking over 500 participants from the US and Europe to rate the costliness of various cultural traditions, such as religious practices, holidays, and family rituals.

14

Which finding, if true, would most directly support the researchers' claim?

(A) The expense associated with a tradition serves as a barrier to entry for outsiders, reinforcing its significance within a particular group

(B) A tradition that requires minimal effort, such as storytelling, could still be passed down from one generation to the next.

(C) The cost of maintaining a cultural tradition can be a limiting factor in its longevity.

(D) The value of a cultural tradition does not necessarily depend on the resources required to maintain it.

The financial crisis that occurred in the years 2007 and 2008 was a time of immense financial instability, marked by the most serious financial downturn since the Great Depression of the 1920s and 1930s. As some economists have contended, the severity of the crisis may have been exacerbated by the repeal of the Glass-Steagall legislation, which represented a set of provisions aimed at constraining banks from consolidating their commercial and proprietary operations. The repeal of this legislation, according to some experts, allowed banks to undertake excessive risks in the market, resulting in the catastrophic economic ramifications of the crisis.

15

Which of the following choices most effectively illustrates the claim of the experts?

(A) The Glass-Steagall legislation prevented traditional banks from making highly risky investments.

(B) A number of the provisions of the Glass-Steagall legislation were repealed in 1999.

(C) Some top economists believe that the Glass-Steagall legislation would not have prevented the activities that led to the financial crisis of 2007-2008.

(D) The Glass-Steagall provisions were part of the 1933 Banking Act and gave banks one year to separate their commercial and proprietary operations.

Section 1, Module 2: Reading and Writing

Directions ⌄

32:00
Hide

Annotate   More

Neanderthals thrived for around 250,000 years throughout Europe and Western Asia by successfully adapting to various environments in which they lived. Scholars typically compare these early settlers to the Inuit of _____ of people residing at the northernmost edge of the human range.

16

Which choice completes the text so that it conforms to the conventions of Standard English?

(A) today groups

(B) today—groups

(C) today; groups

(D) today. Groups

SCORE SHAKE

Back   Next

Section 1, Module 2: Reading and Writing

Directions ⌄

32:00
Hide

Annotate   More

In his painting, Bradford depicted vessels barely visible on the horizon, each _____ in the bay's tranquil water. The sun is low on the horizon, turning the sky from blues to gold to oranges and bouncing a dazzling yellow off the sea.

17

Which choice completes the text so that it conforms to the conventions of Standard English?

(A) mirror

(B) mirrors

(C) mirrored

(D) will mirror

SCORE SHAKE

Back   Next

The mechanical pencil, masterfully designed to eliminate the need for incessant sharpening and featuring an ingenious lead-advancement mechanism, which deftly enables users to effortlessly extend or retract the graphite core, nestled within a _____ the ranks of popularity, securing its place as an indispensable writing instrument in modern times.

18

Which choice completes the text so that it conforms to the conventions of Standard English?

(A) sleek, durable casing. It has swiftly ascended

(B) sleek, durable casing, swiftly ascending

(C) sleek, durable casing, has swiftly ascended

(D) sleek durable casing has swiftly ascended

In 1986, a group of chefs, journalists, and sociologists spearheaded a Slow Food movement, declaring loyalty to unhurried enjoyment. From its beginning, the movement _____ the standardization of taste that fast food chains promote.

19

Which choice completes the text so that it conforms to the conventions of Standard English?

(A) had opposed

(B) opposes

(C) will oppose

(D) has opposed

Section 1, Module 2: Reading and Writing

Annotate   More

A study published by Rice University geoscientist Ming Tang in 2019 offers a new explanation for the origin of Earth's _____ structures called arcs, towering ridges that form when a dense oceanic plate subducts under a less dense continental plate, melts in the mantle below, and then rises and bursts through the continental crust above.

20

Which choice completes the text so that it conforms to the conventions of Standard English?

- (A) continents geological
- (B) continents: geological
- (C) continents; geological
- (D) continents. Geological

Section 1, Module 2: Reading and Writing

Annotate   More

The Amargasaurus, a relatively small sauropod dinosaur, roamed the Earth during the Early Cretaceous period. Its distinct features make it a truly unique _____ short tail equipped with defensive weaponry; and a compact body size, a stark contrast to its massive relatives, perfect for maneuverability. This fascinating creature continues to captivate paleontologists and dinosaur enthusiasts alike.

21

Which choice completes the text so that it conforms to the conventions of Standard English?

- (A) specimen: elongated spines along the neck adorned with a sail-like structure; a relatively
- (B) specimen, elongated spines along the neck adorned with a sail-like structure, a relatively
- (C) specimen elongated spines along the neck adorned with a sail-like structure, a relatively
- (D) specimen; elongated spines along the neck adorned, with a sail-like structure; a relatively

Composed of simple forms, such as a portico of tall square columns and a rectangular beam, the Truman Building has an austere beauty, _____ also can seem cold and imposing. How could the State Department present a friendly face to the world with its new museum while also maintaining the building's architectural character?

22

Which choice completes the text so that it conforms to the conventions of Standard English?

- Ⓐ but
- Ⓑ it
- Ⓒ however, it
- Ⓓ but it

Schematic knowledge helps us reconstruct things we cannot remember. It summarizes the broad pattern of our experience and explains what's typical or ordinary in a given situation. Therefore, any reliance on schematic knowledge will be shaped by this information about what's "normal." _____ if there are things we don't notice while viewing a situation or event, our schematic knowledge will lead us to fill in these "gaps" with knowledge about what's generally in place in that setting.

23

Which choice completes the text with the most logical transition?

- Ⓐ Nevertheless
- Ⓑ Thus,
- Ⓒ Rather,
- Ⓓ On the contrary,

"Monumental" is a word that comes very close to expressing the primary characteristic of Egyptian art. Many modern structures exceed those of Egypt in terms of purely physical size; however, massiveness has nothing to do with monumentality. _____ an Egyptian sculpture no bigger than a person's hand is more monumental than that gigantic pile of stones that constitutes the war memorial in Leipzig. Monumentality is not a matter of external weight but of "inner weight."

24

Which choice completes the text with the most logical transition?

- (A) As such,
- (B) Still
- (C) For example,
- (D) Rather,

When asked whether they are parents who tend to stick to their guns too much or give in too quickly, praise or criticize their children too much, be overprotective or grant excessive freedom, and push their children too hard or not hard enough, shares ranging from 34% to 53% say neither option best describes their parenting style. _____ more than four-in-ten parents (45%) say they tend to be overprotective, compared with 20% who admit to providing too much freedom.

25

Which choice completes the text with the most logical transition?

- (A) As such,
- (B) Indeed,
- (C) For example,
- (D) Nevertheless,

While researching a topic, a student has taken the following notes:

- Sponges and hydra are multicellular animals that live underwater.
- Hydras, which are invertebrates, are found in freshwater environments.
- Sessile animals such as sponges and hydra remain attached to a solid object.
- Both animals reproduce through sexual and asexual means.
- Most sponges, which are invertebrates, are marine animals found in different layers of the ocean.

26

The student wants to emphasize the difference between sponges and hydra. Which choice most effectively uses relevant information from the notes to accomplish this goal?

(A) Hydras are multicellular invertebrate animals.

(B) Sponges and hydras, which live underwater, are sessile.

(C) Sponges are found in different layers of the ocean, and hydras are found in freshwater environments.

(D) Hydras and sponges, which remain attached to a solid object, reproduce through sexual and asexual means.

A teacher has taken the following notes:

- Unlike other kinds of music, tonal music depends on the use of key centers.
- In the early 20th century, composers began to move away from tonal music.
- The music composed in the 1930s by Arnold Schoenberg was not tonal.
- Schoenberg's music from this period is called "12-tone."
- Schoenberg's 12-tone music influenced many composers.
- 12-tone music was not popular with most audiences.

27

The student wants to explain how Schoenberg's music from the 1930s differs from tonal music. Which choice most effectively uses relevant information from the notes to accomplish this goal?

(A) Schoenberg's music was influential without being popular with most audiences.

(B) Composers in the early 20th century began to move away from the use of key centers.

(C) Music that wasn't tonal influenced many composers in the 20th century.

(D) 12-tone music does not depend on the use of key centers.

No.	Answer	Question Type
		TEST 5 Module 1
1	B	Text Completion
2	A	Text Completion
3	C	Text Completion
4	A	Text Completion
5	B	Main Purpose
6	C	Main Idea / Poem
7	C	Main Idea
8	D	Function
9	C	Direct Comprehension
10	A	Cross-Text
11	B	Command of Evidence / Literature
12	C	Command of Evidence / Quantitative
13	A	Command of Evidence / Textual
14	B	Inference
15	D	Conventions of Standard English
16	B	Conventions of Standard English
17	B	Conventions of Standard English
18	C	Conventions of Standard English
19	A	Conventions of Standard English
20	C	Conventions of Standard English
21	C	Transition
22	A	Transition
23	C	Transition
24	B	Transition
25	B	Note Summary
26	D	Note Summary
27	C	Note Summary

No.	Answer	Question Type
		TEST 5 Module 2
1	C	Text Completion
2	B	Text Completion
3	D	Text Completion
4	A	Text Completion
5	B	Function / Poem
6	D	Main Idea / Poem
7	A	Main Idea
8	D	Vocab in Context
9	B	Cross-text
10	D	Command of Evidence / Quantitative
11	B	Command of Evidence / Quantitative
12	B	Command of Evidence / Textual
13	C	Command of Evidence / Literature
14	A	Command of Evidence / Textual
15	A	Command of Evidence / Textual
16	B	Conventions of Standard English
17	C	Conventions of Standard English
18	C	Conventions of Standard English
19	D	Conventions of Standard English
20	B	Conventions of Standard English
21	A	Conventions of Standard English
22	D	Conventions of Standard English
23	B	Transition
24	C	Transition
25	D	Transition
26	C	Note Summary
27	D	Note Summary

DIGITAL SAT Advanced SCORING CHART
Raw score to Score Conversion Chart

Raw Score	Score		Incorrect	Score
54	800		26	530
53	770		25	530
52	740		24	510
51	730		23	510
50	710		22	490
49	710		21	480
48	690		20	480
47	680		19	460
46	680		18	450
45	670		17	430
44	660		16	400
43	650		15	380
42	630		14	360
41	630		13	340
40	620		12	330
39	620		11	310
38	620		10	300
37	610		9	280
36	600		8	260
35	600		7	260
34	590		6	250
33	590		5	240
32	580		4	220
31	580		3	200
30	570		2	200
29	560		1	200
28	550		0	200
27	540